"All sailors face risks, have always faced risks. But none more so than submariners."

— Dr. Robert D. Ballard, from the Introduction

BY SPENCER DUNMORE

Introduction by **Dr. Robert D. Ballard** / Technical Consultant: **J. David Perkins**
Featuring contemporary underwater photographs by **Jonathan Blair** and **Brian Skerry**

CHARTWELL
BOOKS, INC.

A CHARTWELL BOOKS / MADISON PRESS BOOK

LOSTSUBS

This edition is published in 2007 by Chartwell Books, Inc.
A Division of BOOK SALES, INC.
114 Northfield Avenue
Edison, New Jersey 08837
USA

ISBN-13: 978-0-7858-2226-7
ISBN-10: 0-7858-2226-7

Printed and bound in China

Produced by
Madison Press Books
1000 Yonge Street, Suite 200
Toronto, Ontario, Canada
M4W 2K2

Page 1: *Up the Conning Tower*
by artist Stephen Bone.

Pages 2–3: German war
painter Claus Bergen depicts
a U-boat on the prowl in the
North Atlantic.

Pages 4–5: A diver
approaches the conning
tower of the *U-352*, sunk off
the North Carolina coast.
Photograph by Brian Skerry.

Page 7: The wreck of the
Japanese submarine *I-52*,
shot by Jonathan Blair for
National Geographic.

Page 8: *On the Deck of
a German U-boat* by
Claus Bergen.

Contents

Introduction: **The Silent Service**

Everyone in the control van fell silent as images of twisted metal began appearing on the video monitors. We knew that our research ship was now over the grave of the USS *Thresher*. It was the summer of 1984 and we were on a classified mission for the US Navy to photograph the remains of the Cold War nuclear submarine whose disappearance twenty-one years before had taken the lives of 129 men. With most lost ships, a trail of debris leads you to the wreck. But here there was no wreck, just debris. The *Thresher* looked as if it had literally been shredded — crushed by some giant, unseen hand.

A year later, we explored the site of another of the lost submarines featured in this book, the USS *Scorpion*, which lies 11,500 feet below the Atlantic. Unlike the *Thresher*, the *Scorpion* was largely intact — although it had broken almost in two, and the water pressure had jammed its broken tail section inward like a collapsing telescope.

Both of these wreck sites were haunting. It was like visiting a battlefield or the *Arizona* Memorial at Pearl Harbor. You sensed that something truly terrible had happened there and that many people had died. All sailors face risks, have always faced risks. But none more so than submariners.

I have spent most of my adult life around submarines of one kind or another. For thirty-four years, I served in the US Navy and its reserve and worked closely with the submarine forces and made many dives on military submarines. In fact, I lived underwater for almost a month aboard the navy's small atomic submarine *NR-1* when we explored the Reykjanes Ridge, south of Iceland, in 1984. But most of my time has been spent in even smaller subs like the three-person *Alvin* in which I made many dives during my years at the Woods Hole Oceanographic Institution. It was *Alvin* that took me down to the *Titanic* in 1986,

allowing me to be the first human to see her up close in over seventy years. Another minisub, *Delta*, enabled us to explore the most famous ship ever sunk by a submarine, the *Lusitania*.

Yet for me or for any submariner, as we descend into the darkness below the surface, we must, if we are honest, acknowledge how fragile we are in this world. Simply put, we don't belong there. It's a world that wants to kill you and it can be a silent, invisible killer.

All of the lost submarines that lie on the ocean floor — from poor, primitive *Hunley* to the atomic submarine *Kursk* — have incurred a sacrifice of human lives. But each disaster has also played a role in the development of a technology that now allows us to explore the hostile environment that comprises most of this planet. It is this story that is chronicled so well here in Spencer Dunmore's engaging text and through the many fascinating photographs, paintings and diagrams.

Whether these submarines were lost in war or in peace, whether they were Russian or American, British, Australian, German or Japanese, all share in common the outstanding men who served on them. Like aviators, submariners from different navies have more in common with one another than they do with members of their own fleets who sail on the ocean's surface.

These remarkable men (and now women), despite how advanced their submarines have become, will always to some extent be forced to rely upon fortune or God — who, in the words of the Navy Hymn, "bidd'st the mighty ocean deep / Its own appointed limits keep." It is these submariners we should keep in mind as we read this book.

— Dr. Robert D. Ballard
Mystic, Connecticut, April 2002

Prologue: **August 12, 2000**

The sound reverberates through the submarine like a mighty sledgehammer. A shattering, overwhelming din that seems to squash the very air. Some of the startled crewmen immediately think "Collision!" — although that hardly seems possible. Their vessel, after all, is the mighty *Kursk*, pride of the post-Soviet navy, the most modern submarine ever produced by Russian shipyards. How could something so superb be involved in something so mundane?

Nearby, aboard American, British and Norwegian vessels, acoustics operators wince at the sounds jarring in their headphones. But worse, far worse, is still to come. Exactly two minutes and fifteen seconds after the first explosion comes the second. It is more than one hundred times the strength of the first. It registers 3.5 on seismographs more than three thousand miles away — the equivalent of twelve *tons* of TNT exploding.

Fire purges the enormous forward compartment in a literal flash. The heat is so intense — nearly six *thousand* degrees Fahrenheit — that it vaporizes flesh. The force of the explosion reduces the vessel's entire front section to a twisted heap of steel.

The men in the *Kursk*'s second compartment — Captain Gennady Lyachin and most of his senior staff — die instantly. The third compartment, occupied by the chart cabin and the chemical control unit, fares no better. Everyone perishes. As do the twelve men in the fourth compartment — victims of the intense heat and pressure that burst in through bulkhead after bulkhead, ripping equipment from the floor and sides like so many twigs in a storm.

The *Kursk* is mortally wounded. Her thin outer hull has been pierced by an eighty-foot-long gash that extends to the fin. Her tough inner hull, intended to resist the pressure of the deep ocean, is even more heavily damaged. As torrents of seawater flood in, she spirals downward, her reactors shutting off automatically. She is out of control. In her aft compartments, the surviving crewmen are tossed about, flung from side to side as the stricken submarine plummets. She smashes into the seabed and carves a trail nearly five hundred feet long in the sand before coming to rest, nose down, angled twenty degrees to port. The surface is 354 feet above.

Four minutes have elapsed since the first explosion.

Twenty-three crewmembers are still alive. They cram themselves into the ninth compartment, location of the *Kursk*'s after escape chamber. Scared, apprehensive, some are injured, many have bloody ears from burst eardrums. Numbly they stare at one another, every man trying to come to grips with the horrific reality.

Already, the wan light provided by the emergency power system is starting to dim. Soon it will be totally dark in the submarine. A man sobs quietly; another scribbles on a scrap of paper. Water continues to trickle in. Is it coming in faster than a few minutes ago? As the atmosphere within the sub

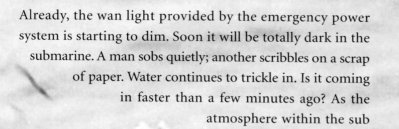

deteriorates,
blinding headaches
start to affect the men. Some
are losing consciousness, their heads lolling
into the seawater that steadily fills the compartment.

The end is near.

Despite the technical excellence of their craft, with its state-of-the-art systems and equipment, its two nuclear reactors, its double hull with a ten-foot gap in between to house guided missiles, its four-inch layer of thick rubber coating to deaden any sonar echoes, the crew still faces the same hazards that faced submersible pioneers eons ago. The same implacably hostile environment. And the same total dependence upon complex systems. It is the lot of every submariner. It always has been.

Chapter One: **The Birth of the Submarine**

No one knows who it was. No one knows when it happened. Or even where. But it is certain that at a distant point in misty antiquity, someone looked into a pond or into the sea and mused, "A boat that could travel under the water, instead of on it, would be a formidable weapon of war."

A sage observation. The truth of it fired the imagination of scores of inventors over the generations. To travel beneath the surface is to travel invisibly. But underwater travel and combat posed substantial technical challenges, as centuries of experimenters would discover.

Some claim Alexander the Great was the world's first submariner. The Macedonian conqueror is said to have studied underwater life from a glass barrel that may have qualified as a submarine. Over the centuries, many others experimented with underwater craft propelled by oars or wiggling fishlike tails. In 1696, French scientist Denis Papin built a submersible that introduced some of the elements of the modern submarine — including a ballast tank, a bilge pump and an air pipe to the surface. It underwent at least one successful test.

The first real attempt to use a submarine militarily came in 1776 during the American War of Independence. A young man by the name of David Bushnell decided to strike a blow for liberty by sinking a British ship with his egg-shaped submersible, the *Turtle*. Built of wood, Bushnell's boat was equipped with hand-operated propellers — one for guiding the craft up or down, and another for moving it forward or backward. One foot pump let in water to make the submarine dive, another expelled it for surfacing. Seven hundred pounds of lead ballast kept the little craft upright. The plan was for the *Turtle* to approach her target awash, then dive beneath its hull. The intrepid — and busy — operator would then bore a hole in the hull and attach a 150-pound explosive charge and a clockwork timer that could be set in motion by pulling a cord.

(Opposite) The nuclear-powered submarine USS *Maryland* plows through the water during its sea trials in 1992. Five hundred and sixty feet long, the vessel is ten times the length of America's first submarine, the USS *Holland*, purchased by the US Navy in 1900.

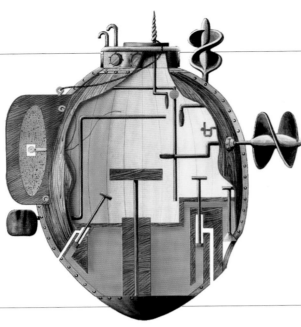

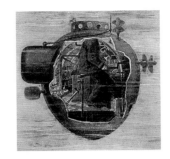

The **Turtle**

David Bushnell's *Turtle* heads for safer waters after detonating its explosives in New York Harbor in September 1776 (below). The egg-shaped submersible, which normally floated with about six inches of its body exposed above the surface, relied on two crude propellers for navigation. The large screw projecting from its hatch (diagram, left) was used for drilling into the hull of an enemy ship so that explosives could be attached. Frustratingly, the screw could not penetrate the copper-sheathed bottom of the British warship HMS *Eagle* (below, at right).

The man originally designated to undertake this hazardous mission was Bushnell's brother. He fell ill — possibly at the thought of what lay ahead — and another volunteer was found: a doughty individual, Sergeant Ezra Lee of the Continental Army. Under cover of darkness on September 6, 1776, Lee set off to attack HMS *Eagle*, the flagship of Admiral Howe, which was then blockading New York. Lee was spotted by the British, and boats were soon in hot pursuit. Thinking quickly, Lee detonated the explosives intended for the *Eagle* and got away in the subsequent confusion. Two more attempts were made to sink British warships; neither succeeded. Britannia still ruled the waves, although the Americans won their independence.

Another American, Robert Fulton, became one of the major figures in the development of the submarine — although he is better remembered for his pioneering work on the steamboat. Like so many of his successors, he was of Irish ancestry and apparently dedicated to ridding Ireland of the British. But he had no wish to kill Englishmen. His idea was to use the submarine as a means of neutralizing the warship, the "ultimate weapon" of the day. Fulton reasoned that if England's warships were rendered impotent, Britain would lose much of her international power. His first submarine, completed in 1801, was the *Nautilus*. Twenty-one feet long, with a hand-cranked propeller and a copper outer skin, she was the world's first submersible to have separate methods of propulsion for travel above and below the water. She also became the first to embody a form of conning tower, a hemispherical protrusion made of metal. A spike was provided to secure *Nautilus* to the intended target while the explosive charge — then referred to as a "torpedo" — was attached. The submersible had a crew of three and was equipped with horizontal and vertical rudders.

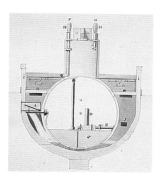

(Above) A cross section of the *Nautilus* showing interior chambers for crew, ballast and submarine bombs. (Right) Robert Fulton directs the *Nautilus* during trials in the Seine estuary in 1801.

On June 3, 1801, in the Seine estuary, the *Nautilus* demonstrated her capabilities, descending to about twenty-four feet and remaining underwater for an hour. Fulton then added bottled compressed air to his submarine, increasing her underwater endurance to a reported five hours. Another test followed, in which the *Nautilus* — submerged the entire time — sank an old schooner in Brest Harbor with a twenty-pound gunpowder charge. It was an impressive demonstration. Unfortunately for Fulton, the local prefect feared reprisals and refused him permission to mount any more mock attacks. Furthermore, the French government rejected his proposal for an improved *Nautilus*, claiming that submarine warfare was furtive and unworthy of French arms.

WILLS'S CIGARETTES.

THE NAUTILUS

Fulton gave up on the French and, swallowing his anti-British feelings, headed across the Channel in 1804. At the time, rumors claimed that Bonaparte was preparing to invade England. The prime minister, William Pitt, wanted to find out if Fulton's submersible could be of value at this time of national danger. He appointed a commission to study the matter. But the Lords of the Admiralty — still heady after Nelson's victory at Trafalgar — turned up their aristocratic noses at Fulton's idea. Lurking in the depths and attacking ships unseen was no way for the Royal Navy to fight a war! Undeterred, Fulton returned to the United States in 1806 and, four years later, talked Congress into putting up five thousand dollars to finance the development of a steam-powered submarine. A prototype was started — more than eighty feet long, with a beam of twenty-one feet — but Fulton died in 1815, before it could be completed, and the project was abandoned.

Others followed in Fulton's wake. In England, a former seafaring man named Thomas Johnstone designed a clockwork-powered submarine made of iron and lined with cork and wood. He wanted to proceed with a full-scale prototype, but the tightfisted Lords of the Admiralty refused to finance the project. To add to his discomfiture, Johnstone was arrested in 1817 on suspicion of working for the French and the Americans; one rumor had it that the French wanted him to build a submarine capable of rescuing Napoleon from exile on St. Helena.

Almost fifty years would pass before a submarine would be used as a weapon of war. And it would be during a different kind of warfare, on the other side of the Atlantic.

Fulton's *Nautilus* may not have won over French government officials or the British Admiralty, but his invention captured the public imagination. (Left) A fanciful rendering of the *Nautilus* graces a period cigarette card. (Opposite) Other bold inventors followed in Fulton's wake. (Top) Brutus de Villeroi's *Alligator*, built in 1861 for the US Navy, was forty-six feet long and featured an enormous hand-cranked propeller. Ironically, it, like the Confederate submarine *Hunley*, was intended for use in Charleston Harbor — but it was lost under tow off Cape Hatteras. (Bottom) Frenchmen Charles Burn and Simon Bourgeois fared no better with *Le Plongeur*. Despite its sleek design and formidable size, the 140-foot-long submersible proved too unstable for the French Navy.

Chapter Two: **The First Underwater Weapon of War**

Service on the Confederate States Ship (CSS) *H.L. Hunley* was not for the faint of heart. Eight men sat hunched inside what was essentially an overgrown boiler — roughly forty feet long, four feet high and four feet wide — constructed of riveted iron plates. Sweating in the darkness, they worked the massive squeaking crank that turned her single propeller. At her bow crouched the captain, peering out through the small glass view ports in the stubby conning tower. Close at hand was the lever he used to manipulate the diving planes and the wheel with which he controlled the rudder. A depth gauge and compass completed his instrumentation. A flickering candle provided the illumination, such as it was.

The *Hunley* had been launched in July 1863 to help break the Union blockade that was slowly strangling the ports of the South during the American Civil War. By December of that year, it had succeeded only in killing almost every member of the two separate crews that had bravely stepped forth to man her. This grim tally included her hapless inventor and namesake, Horace L. Hunley, who had been in command of the sub during a test run. A valve in the forward ballast tank had been left open and the ill-fated vessel sank, nose down, into the muddy bottom of Charleston's Cooper River. Divers salvaged the vessel and recovered the bodies of the unfortunate crew.

While many in the Confederate camp considered the "submarine torpedo boat" a death trap, there were still men who were eager to serve on her. Perhaps this time, the *Hunley* would be lucky. Lieutenant George Dixon, a member of the 21st Alabama Volunteers, was appointed commander of

The CSS *Hunley*, depicted below in a painting by Conrad Wise Chapman, was equipped with ballast tanks at each end that could be flooded by valves or emptied by hand pumps.

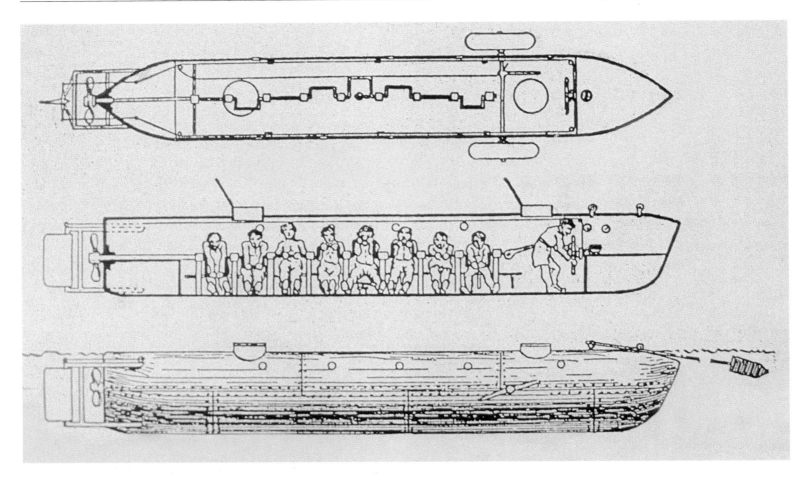

(Above) These later sketches of the *Hunley* were made by Simon Lake for *McLures Magazine* in 1899 and were based on a description by a crewmember who had survived the submersible's first sinking. In November 2001, archaeologists examining the remains of the *Hunley* announced conclusively that there were only eight — not nine — men aboard the submarine during its last voyage. (Far left) A cross section of the *Hunley*, based on sketches by William A. Alexander, who directed her construction. (Left) Horace L. Hunley.

the troubled submarine and quickly assembled an enthusiastic new crew in late December, 1863. Little did these recruits know that they were about to make submarining history.

The *Hunley* soon had its first test under combat conditions, and it happened at night. The submersible set out towing a "torpedo," a copper cylinder containing ninety pounds of explosives. The idea was to dive under a likely target, dragging the torpedo behind, but strong currents in the entrance to Charleston Harbor made it impossible to control the weapon. Dixon was well aware of the very real danger of being sunk by his own torpedo — a danger that still haunts submariners today. The *Hunley* moved cautiously among the Union vessels, surfacing and diving repeatedly as the enemy's calcium lights swept over the black waters. Dixon became particularly concerned about fatigue among his crew. Turning the massive crank was exhausting work, even for the stalwart young men inside the *Hunley*. As it happened, Dixon's concerns were well-founded. By the time the submarine was in position to launch an attack, the crew was completely drained.

Charleston under Siege

The defiant city of Charleston (above) played a crucial role in the Civil War, even before the first shots were fired at Fort Sumter in 1861. It was at Charleston that South Carolina officials voted for secession from the Union — and it was in the waters around the city's harbor that Confederate and Union forces waged the fiercest naval battles of the Civil War. Shortly after the attack on Fort Sumter, the US Navy instigated a massive blockade around Charleston Harbor in hopes of choking off the city's supply lines. The sloop of war USS *Housatonic* joined the blockade in late 1862. However, despite repeated assaults on the city by army and navy, Confederate resistance remained strong. In the spring and summer of 1863, the US Navy assembled the largest fleet of ironclads the world had ever seen and mounted a fierce attack against the rebels near Fort Sumter. Hoping for capitulation, the US Navy succeeded only in fuelling the Confederates' hatred for the enemy and strengthening their resolve.

A few days later, following a terrifying incident in which the towed torpedo became entangled in the *Hunley*'s rudder, Dixon decided to affix the missile to the end of a spar protruding from the submarine's bow. This new harpoon-type torpedo would have to be rammed into the intended target, then detonated at the tug of a lanyard — once the crew had reversed the propeller and backed the submersible a safe distance away.

By mid-January, Dixon and his crew had moved in closer on the blockading Union fleet. William Alexander, who had helped develop the *Hunley* and served for a time as Dixon's engineering officer, later described the method he and Dixon formulated for their attack: "The plan was

to take the bearings of the ships as they took position for the night, steer for one of them, keeping about six feet under water, coming occasionally to the surface for air and observation, and when nearing the vessel, come to the surface for final observation before striking her, which was to be done under the counter, if possible."

By early February, the submarine's crew was trained and ready. And now a new arrival caught Dixon's attention: the 207-foot-long USS *Housatonic*, rocking gently at anchor a mere three miles from Battery Marshall, where the *Hunley* was moored. The young Confederate commander resolved to attack her as soon as conditions were suitable.

On February 17, 1864, as day gave way to a frigid but clear evening, Dixon and several of his men made their way to the mouth of the Breach Inlet, where they took a last compass bearing on their target. Union sailors aboard the federal vessel had been forewarned about the *Hunley*, thanks to two deserters from the Confederate cause who had stolen across Union lines in a rowboat. *Housatonic*'s commander, Captain Charles W. Pickering, had ordered his officers to keep "a vigilant lookout, glasses in constant use…." At the first sign of trouble, the chains were to be slipped and the gong sounded. Twenty-five pounds of steam were to be kept up throughout the night so that the ship was always ready for departure.

(Left) A wash drawing of the USS *Housatonic* by R.G. Skerrett. (Opposite, top) The *Hunley* underwater as it advances toward the *Housatonic*, a torpedo attached to its spar. (Bottom left) A period diagram of Singer's Torpedo, used in the attack on the *Housatonic*. (Bottom right) Side and overhead views of the *Hunley*.

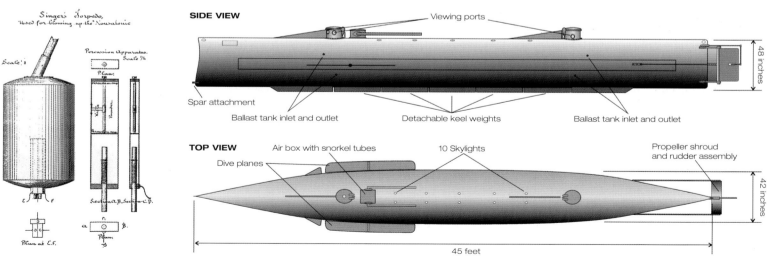

Singer's Torpedo,
used for blowing up the Housatonic

Scale: 3

Percussion Apparatus.
Scale 1/6

Plan at E.F.

Section A.B. Section C.D.

SIDE VIEW

Viewing ports

48 inches

Spar attachment

Ballast tank inlet and outlet

Detachable keel weights

Ballast tank inlet and outlet

TOP VIEW

Air box with snorkel tubes

10 Skylights

Propeller shroud
and rudder assembly

Dive planes

42 inches

45 feet

As the pale light of a full moon filled the cloudless night sky, Dixon hesitated briefly. Unless cloud materialized, the *Hunley*'s approach would certainly not go unnoticed. Nevertheless, he decided to proceed with the mission. He squeezed himself through the narrow forward hatch of the sub and lit the candle. In the dim metallic tube of a hull, he could see his men taking their positions at the crankshaft. He nodded to them and they began the exhausting task of getting the submarine into motion. The laboring crew could see nothing but they could hear the water sloshing against the hull and the crank squeaking as it turned. After a few minutes, Dixon came up for air and a check of his position. The iron propeller shaft complained as it turned in its metal collar. Directly ahead, the sloop lay at anchor, looking enormous and threatening as the ungainly submarine approached, wallowing in the choppy waters, the glow of the candle just visible through the tiny view ports.

South Carolina artist Daniel Dowdey re-creates the *Hunley*'s attack on the *Housatonic*. (Above) A quick check of position. (Opposite, top) After ramming the torpedo into the hull of the Union warship, the crew frantically cranks in reverse to set the *Hunley* free. (Opposite, bottom) With a yank of the cord, the torpedo explodes.

Union sailors aboard the sloop spotted the submarine heading their way. They raised the alarm and opened fire, their bullets ricocheting off the iron hull and smacking into the water. Dixon ignored the gunfire. He held the wheel on course, grimly waiting out the last few seconds before contact. The sloop seemed to swell as he neared it, a menacing shape, black and frightening. Soon it filled every square inch of his view port, as if the world suddenly consisted of nothing else.

Dixon probably let out a high-pitched rebel yell in the instant before the barbed torpedo head drove into the ship's timbers. He had done so scores of times during practice runs, with the crew enthusiastically joining in. This was the supreme moment, the culmination of countless days of training.

As the torpedo made contact, the *Hunley* came to a jarring halt. Immediately, the sweating sailors started to reverse the crank to pull their vessel free. A member of the *Housatonic*'s crew, Ensign Charles Craven, recalled: "I heard the Officer of the Deck give the order, 'Call all hands to Quarters.' I went on deck and saw something in the water on the starboard side of the ship, about thirty feet off, and the Captain and the Executive Officer were firing at it. I fired two shots at her with my revolver as she was standing toward the ship as soon as I saw her, and a third shot when she was almost under the counter, having to lean over the port to fire it.

"I then went to my division, which is the second, and consists of four broadside thirty-two-pounder guns in the waist, and tried with the captain of number six gun to train it on this object as she was backing from the ship, and about forty or fifty feet off by then. I had nearly succeeded, and was almost about to pull the lock string when the explosion took place."

The torpedo had set off gunpowder in the *Housatonic*'s aft

(Left) As the *Housatonic* sinks in the distance, the triumphant Confederate sub pauses briefly to savor victory. Dowdey's painting supports the more recent theory about the *Hunley*'s final moments, based on reports from *Housatonic* survivors — that whatever eventually happened to the sub, it survived the assault on the *Housatonic* and a subsequent volley of gunfire from officers aboard the sinking vessel. According to eyewitnesses, it was last seen reversing its course and heading for shore. (Opposite) Dowdey's romanticized image of the *Hunley* on the bottom of the harbor.

powder magazine, sending shattering shock waves along the *Hunley*'s iron hull. Every man must have reeled, his head spinning, trying to recover from the awful shock and the numbing din.

The *Housatonic* sagged in the water, abruptly rolling to port, stricken. Water poured into her. Ensign Craven remembered: "I heard a report like the distant firing of a howitzer. The ship went down by the stern, and about three or four minutes after the stern was submerged, the whole ship was submerged." The powerful explosion had torn off the stern of the vessel, killing five of her crew.

For the first time in history, a submarine had sunk an enemy ship. But the *Hunley*'s victory ultimately was bought with the lives of Lieutenant Dixon and his crew. What happened in the minutes and hours after the successful strike on the *Housatonic*? Until the Confederate submarine's historic recovery in August 2000, a number of possible theories had become part of the lore surrounding the *Hunley*. Some speculated that the torpedo's explosion had either seriously damaged or swamped the small craft. Others thought she had been run over by another Union warship, USS *Canandaigua*. Or perhaps swift seas and worsening weather had overwhelmed the exhausted crew. Whatever the cause, the submarine and its eight men never made it back to Battery Marshall.

Both the *Hunley* and the *Housatonic* lay undisturbed off the shores of Charleston for more than a century, about a thousand feet apart. The sloop's wooden hull soon vanished but the *Hunley* endured, thanks to her iron construction.

Beginning in 1981, author Clive Cussler funded two expeditions to search for the lost Confederate submarine using a proton magnetometer and a metal detector. Finally, in 1995, his team — working with the South Carolina Institute of Archaeology and Anthropology — located the wreck buried in the mud at the bottom of Charleston Harbor. She lay on her side, her forward hatch still bolted shut from

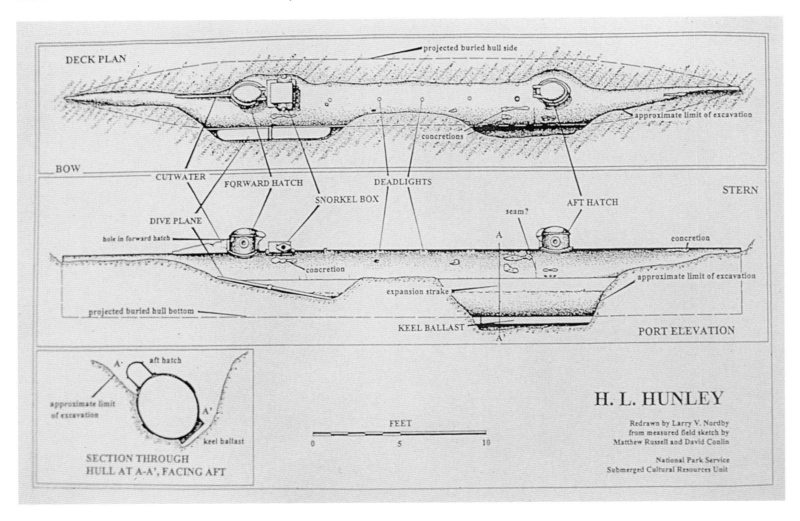

DECK PLAN

projected buried hull side

approximate limit of excavation

concretions

BOW

CUTWATER   FORWARD HATCH   DEADLIGHTS   STERN

SNORKEL BOX   AFT HATCH

DIVE PLANE   seam?

hole in forward hatch   A   concretion

concretion

approximate limit of excavation

projected buried hull bottom

expansion strake

KEEL BALLAST   PORT ELEVATION

aft hatch

approximate limit
of excavation

keel ballast

SECTION THROUGH
HULL AT A-A', FACING AFT

FEET

0   5   10

H. L. HUNLEY

Redrawn by Larry V. Nordby
from measured field sketch by
Matthew Russell and David Conlin

National Park Service
Submerged Cultural Resources Unit

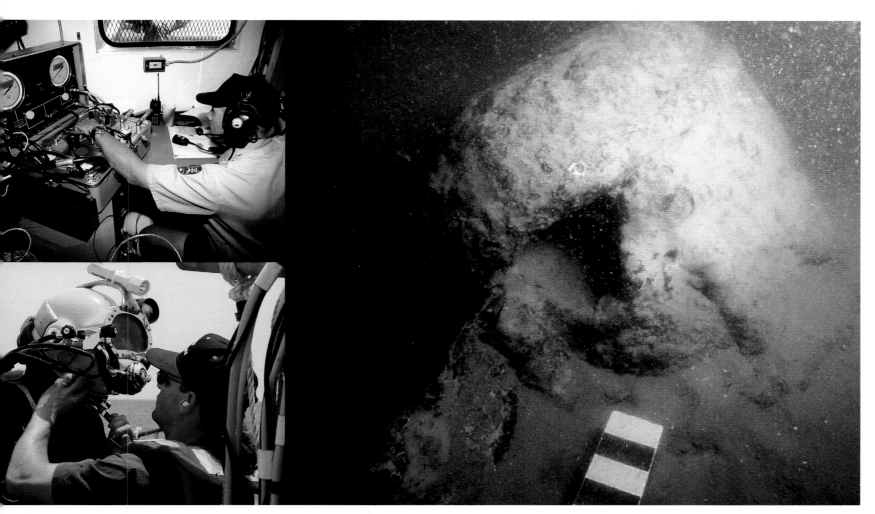

(Opposite) A drawing showing the position of the *Hunley* on the sea floor. (Below right) The forward hatch and cutwater of the *Hunley* during the 1996 assessment. (Below left) Members of the recovery crew.

the inside, her left observation port a gaping, glassless hole — possibly shot out during those desperate last moments before impact. When one of the expedition divers, Ralph Wilbanks, reached inside through the port, he found the vessel completely filled with silt — which raised hopes among the researchers that whatever might be found inside the submarine would be well preserved. Wilbanks also located the submarine's port diving plane. The snorkel mechanism, or air box, was in the "up" position; however, the four-foot-long breathing tubes — fitted with stopcocks so that they could be closed when the submarine dived — had broken off at the elbows.

In August 2000, the *H.L. Hunley* broke surface again for the first time in more than 130 years. In order to raise the submarine, divers had placed thirty-two slings around the sand- and water-filled hull to support its twenty-thousand-pound weight. The loop straps, which were cushioned with inflated foam bags and attached to a steel frame, had cradled the vessel while a crane hoisted the unit to the surface.

Moved to the Warren Lasch Conservation Center on the grounds of the old Charleston Naval Base, the *Hunley* underwent a meticulous examination. Its rusting remains have revealed a treasure trove of secrets. For example, the submarine itself is considerably more advanced than most researchers anticipated, forcing a revision of the commonly held opinions about the South's technical prowess.

Underwater photographer Brian Skerry captured the *Hunley* for *National Geographic* shortly before it was raised from the bottom of Charleston Harbor. (Above) The encrusted remains of the submarine's propeller. (Right) Bright yellow foam bags attached to fabric slings cradle the fragile hull.

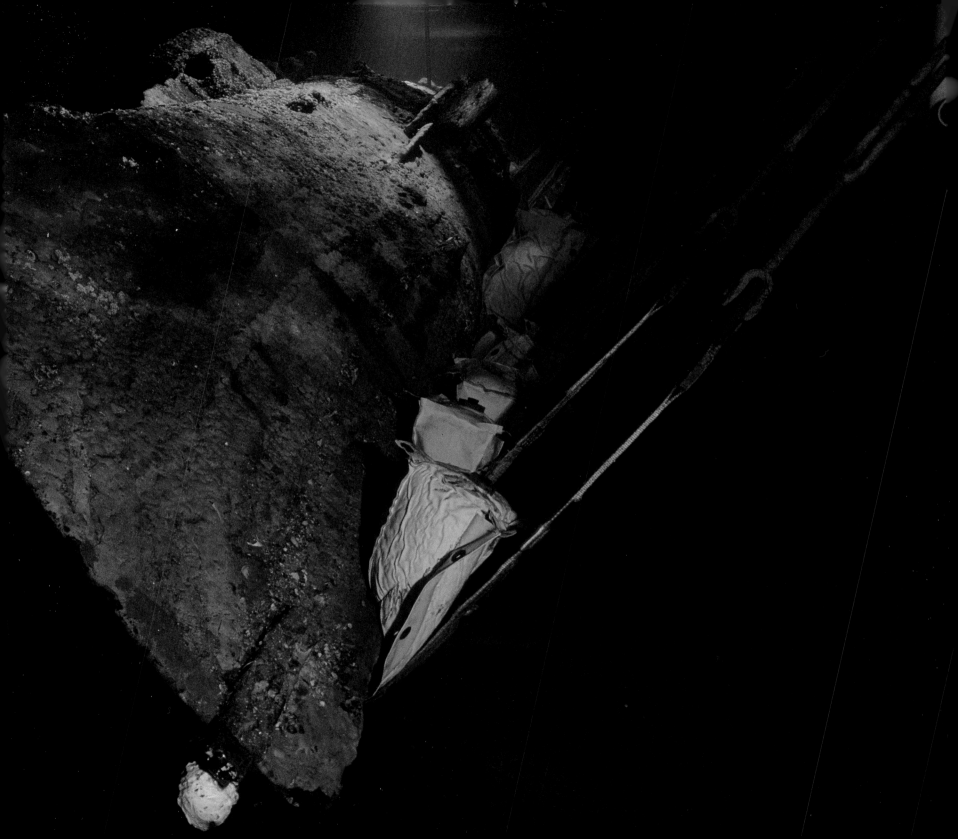

Raising a Fragile Rebel **Ghost**

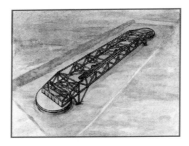

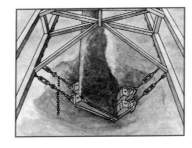

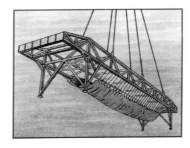

Divers excavated an area approximately 40 feet wide by 130 feet long to expose the top of the submarine. Two massive custom-engineered suction piles were then lowered and positioned into the sediment at either end of the excavation area.

With the suction piles acting as a platform, a recovery frame (truss) was lowered to the wreck by heavy lifting equipment. Divers guided it into position so that it straddled the *Hunley*, then used knives to carefully dig it into the sediment.

Divers exposed the hull, one small section at a time, to determine its condition before positioning the support rigging. A twelve-inch-wide fabric sling, with chains for length adjustment at either end, was draped under each section of exposed hull.

Once all slings were in position, foam was injected into containment bags attached to each sling. These bags provided support for the vessel and conformed to its shape at critical points. Tension straps stabilized the sub in the truss and prevented movement during transit.

The remains of most of the *Hunley*'s eight-man crew have also been found and identified, along with various fragments of clothing and equipment. Several are of particular interest. A bent gold coin is believed to have been the property of the captain, George E. Dixon. It had particular significance for the young officer. According to legend, his girlfriend Queenie Bennett gave him an 1860 twenty-dollar gold coin when he went off to war. In April 1862, at the Battle of Shiloh, the coin saved him from serious injury, possibly death, when it stopped a Union bullet. After this incident, Dixon had the lines *"Shiloh/April 6, 1862/My life preserver/G.E.D."* added to the deformed coin.

Another item is a Union medallion. Made of copper or bronze, the medallion bears the name of a Connecticut soldier who was reported killed during an assault on Battery Wagner, South Carolina, in July 1863. At that time, Union soldiers were not issued dog tags; consequently, many had medallions made so that their bodies could be identified if they were killed in battle. The medallion found inside the *Hunley* has a picture of George Washington on one side; the other bears the name of the soldier, Ezra Chamberlin, and his unit, Company K, Regiment 7 of the Connecticut Volunteers. About the size of a half-dollar, Chamberlin's medallion was apparently worn around the neck of the *Hunley*'s first mate. Was it just a battlefield souvenir? Or did Chamberlin give the medallion to the Confederate sailor with a dying request to notify his family in Connecticut? Alternatively, did Chamberlin survive Battery Wagner, only to die aboard the *Hunley* as a turncoat? Or as a Union spy attempting to sabotage the submarine?

Archaeologists worked from the stern of the submarine forward, examining every fragment of evidence. Among the first items found was a skull and what appeared to be part of a bellows. It is believed the bellows was used to draw fresh air through the snorkel tubes. "It appears to be two wooden pieces with leather between," said project director Robert Neyland. The remains of the crewmen were all found at their stations, indicating that there was no scrambling to get out of the submarine. After the sinking of the *Housatonic*, the submarine turned, signaled its success to the shore, then vanished. A number of artifacts were discovered in the submarine, including an encrusted lantern, which archaeologists removed and X-rayed. Neyland said it was not yet known what fueled the lantern, but it certainly was "unique and sophisticated for its time."

The investigative work on the remains of the *Hunley* continues, and it will still be some time before the complete story of this remarkable chapter in submarine development can be told.

Coin © Friends of the Hunley

(Opposite) The *Hunley* is suspended above a specially constructed metal conservation tank. (Above) Senior archaeologist Maria Jacobsen holds an inscribed gold coin discovered inside the submarine. The bent twenty-dollar gold piece (right) belonged to Lt. George E. Dixon, and its discovery confirms absolutely that Dixon was aboard.

Putting a **Human Face** to the *Hunley*

The sole photograph that for so long gave a face to the captain of the ill-fated Confederate sub is not that of Lt. George Dixon. In October 2001, the Hunley Commission announced that the tintype (detail, left) — given to the Commission by the great-granddaughter of Dixon's sweetheart, Queenie Bennett — had been thoroughly analyzed by a photographic expert as well as by experts at the Museum of the Confederacy and at the South Carolina Institute of Archaeology and Anthropology. The subject's clothing and the furniture in the photograph were carefully examined and proved to be from the post-Civil War period. The *Hunley* sank in 1864.

Luckily, Dixon's skull was among the remains recovered from the submarine. Project archaeologists and conservators, using state-of-the-art technology, will study the skull as they undertake reconstruction of Dixon's face. They will do the same with the seven other skulls that were found and removed.

A number of other relics have been unearthed from the sediment-filled vessel, including (right, top) the mysterious medallion that bears the name of a Union Army volunteer — possibly a spy aboard the *Hunley* — as well as several buttons (right, bottom), a rubber boot, a pencil stub and a pipe (below).

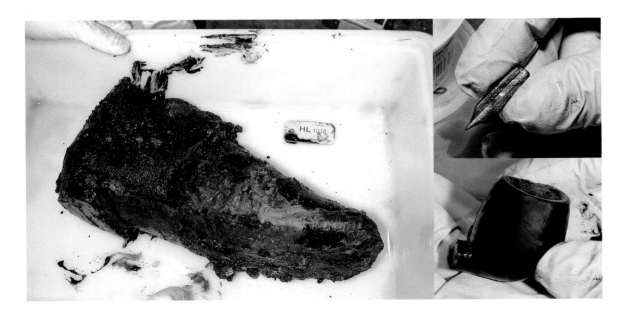

What Sank the *Hunley*?

Since the raising of the *H.L. Hunley* from the muddy bottom of Charleston Harbor, historians have learned much about the construction and operation of the Confederate submarine. But on the question of what actually sank her, they remain in the dark.

The wreck was found pointing in the direction of her base at Sullivan Island, which suggests she survived the sinking of the *Housatonic* and was heading home. This tallies with eyewitness reports from the time of a blue light at the water's surface — the agreed-upon signal that the *Hunley* was to flash to Battery Marshall on the island after the attack, to be answered with a blue light that would guide the submarine back.

The only major damage to the craft reported so far is the missing glass from the left observation port in the forward conning tower — which may have been broken by the blast or by the small-arms fire the *Housatonic*'s crew rained on the sub. Did the *Hunley* then fill with water on the run home? And was the observation port actually shattered that night, or later, during her long years on the bottom? So far, archaeologists have found no traces of glass in the sediment taken from the conning tower — a finding that strengthens the theory that the damage to the port took place before the sinking, not after.

Another theory involves the *Hunley*'s spectacular Achilles' heel, her forward and aft ballast tanks — bizarrely constructed with tops left open to the interior of the submarine. With any serious tilting of the vessel, water would pour out of these tanks into the crew compartment. Perhaps when the *Hunley* was rocked by the aftershock of the *Housatonic*'s explosion — or, as some historians have suspected, when it was knocked off kilter after being rammed by the Union warship *Canandaigua* — water slopped out of the ballast tanks into the rest of the submarine. Trapped below the surface, in negative buoyancy, she wouldn't have been able to pump out the water or control her trim. The crewmen might have cranked frantically as they struggled to reach the surface, or they may have kept her moving forward to supply them with enough air through the breathing pipes. But as they worked, they would have succumbed to anoxia (oxygen starvation) — cranking more and more slowly as they grew drowsy. The *Hunley* would then have settled gently to the bottom.

Of course, given the *Hunley*'s two previous sinkings, the sub may simply have been unlucky yet again — filling with water after an inattentive crewmember allowed the ballast tanks to overflow. In fact, in recent months, the attention has shifted from the craft to her crew. Perhaps an analysis of the men's remains will provide us with some clues. Did they drown or asphyxiate? And can we tell? The results of tests such as these may finally solve the mystery of what sank the *Hunley*.

Chapter Three: **The Submarine Comes of Age**

In the second half of the nineteenth century, the world's navies began to take notice of the submarine. The submersibles may have been dirty, dangerous, malodorous and totally lacking in élan, but there was no denying the advantages they offered. At this point, the one great problem that still dogged submarine development, at least in its military applications, was the lack of a good weapon. Towing barrels packed with explosives was ineffectual. And the so-called spar torpedo — a charge attached to a long harpoonlike pole that the submarine's crew was supposed to ram into an enemy ship — was as dangerous to the submarine as to its target.

The Reverend George Garrett (center, holding his child) and his crew aboard the *Resurgam* after its construction. The *Resurgam*, the world's first successful engine-powered submarine, was lost under tow off Wales in 1880.

This was about to change. In the early 1860s, Robert Whitehead, an English engineer in charge of a marine engineering company at Fiume (now Rijeka, Slovenia), was approached by Captain Giovanni Luppis of the Imperial and Royal Austrian Navy. The Austrians were working on an explosive-carrying motor boat and wanted Whitehead to try his hand at developing a mechanical remote control system for it. Whitehead soon abandoned the idea as impractical, but working on the project gave him the idea for what he termed an "automobile torpedo." His first model was ready by 1866. Driven by a twin-cylinder engine powered by compressed air, Whitehead's torpedo had a range of two hundred yards at a speed of six knots. Further models followed.

In 1870, Whitehead visited Britain at the invitation of the Royal Navy. The Admiralty, after witnessing more than one hundred test firings that culminated in the sinking of an old warship, bought a supply of his torpedoes. The following year, the British government began manufacturing them under license at the Royal Laboratories in Woolwich.

Although Whitehead also developed a tube to fire the torpedo, he didn't view his invention as a submarine weapon. He imagined that torpedoes would be land-based weapons, used to protect harbors from attack. Nevertheless, to him must go much of the credit for the ultimate transformation of the submarine into a viable weapon of war.

Thorsten Nordenfelt's ambitious submarine designs proved popular with the public, as these period illustrations (left and below) show. Although his submersibles had limited success when actually put to the test, they were instrumental in awakening navies around the world to the tremendous potential of submarines as formidable weapons of war.

For the next two decades, numerous inventors in different countries labored away on a variety of submarines, most of them conspicuously unsuccessful. There was George W. Garrett, an English clergyman whose experiments with the boat he named *Resurgam* (Latin for "I shall rise again") earned him a deal for two submarines and a commission in the Ottoman Navy. The Scandinavian inventor Thorsten Nordenfelt caused a sensation when he displayed a 125-foot-long submarine at the 1887 naval review honoring Queen Victoria's Golden Jubilee. He sold his ship on the spot to the Russians. But when it ran aground off Jutland, the deal fell through.

During the 1880s and 1890s, the United States government invited tenders for the construction of experimental submarines for Uncle Sam's consideration. Although at least one of the designs submitted was quite advanced — that of Simon Lake, for a submarine called *Argonaut I* that featured a snorkel and wheels for travelling along the ocean bottom — the navy repeatedly favored the designs of John Philip Holland.

Of all the personalities involved in the development of the submarine, none stands out like John Holland. Like so many of his peers, he was an Irishman who had moved to the United States in 1873

Simon Lake's
Argonaut

Unlike most of his fellow inventors at the time, Simon Lake (right) was not interested in the warlike possibilities of submarines. His first working submersible, *Argonaut I* (above and left), was named after the Argonaut sea creature (similar to a Portuguese man-of-war) that could navigate on and below the surface as well as on the sea floor. The thirty-six-foot *Argonaut I*, built in Baltimore in 1897, boasted a 30 HP gasoline engine and three wheels that allowed it to traverse all kinds of surfaces. In 1898, Lake and a crew of five took it on a successful test run into Chesapeake Bay and along the Atlantic coast — surviving on the fish, clams and oysters that were retrieved through the dive compartment. The *Argonaut* design was the first of many submarines Lake developed for peaceful purposes during a long and distinguished career.

burning with a desire to rid his native land of the British. His plan was to threaten the British fleet with a revolutionary new weapon — the submarine — built in American shipyards. In 1878, with backing from the Fenian Brotherhood, he built the *Fenian Ram*. With a 15 HP Brayton gasoline engine and a crew of three, the *Ram* sported a pneumatic gun that fired a six-foot-long dynamite-filled steel projectile. Although the vessel was a comparative success, Holland's relationship with his Fenian backers was shortlived.

In 1893, the same year that Holland won the US Navy's design competition for a submarine torpedo boat powered by steam, the Holland Torpedo Boat Company was launched. Uneasy about the use of steam in submarines, Holland continued work on a gasoline-powered boat, the *Holland VI* — which combined the electric battery, electric motor and an internal combustion engine. Holland also incorporated a safety tank to impart positive buoyancy in the event of an emergency — a feature still found in today's nuclear submarines. At the navy's suggestion, the sub was fitted with a torpedo tube for launching standard Whitehead torpedoes. On April 11, 1900, the *Holland VI* was bought by the US Navy. Four months later, the navy contracted with the Holland Torpedo Boat Company for a further six submarines to an improved design. This design was the prototype for the first submarines built for the British, Dutch and Japanese navies. The Holland Torpedo Boat Company, today known as the Electric Boat Company, continues to build submarines for the US Navy.

Despite the advances in submarine design by the end of the nineteenth century, the underwater vessels were still far from universally popular in the hidebound Royal Navy. Many officers shied away from serving on the nasty, smelly, hideously claustrophobic things, despite the extra pay on offer by the navy. That gallant old salt, Admiral Sir Arthur Wilson, VC, considered the submarine "underhand, unfair and damned un-English." He recommended that in wartime, captured submarine crews should be hanged without trial. A more balanced opinion came from Sir John "Jackie" Fisher, Britain's charismatic First Sea Lord and father of the modern battleship. Fisher declared that the submarine would effect an "immense impending revolution." He was soon proved correct.

(Above) John Holland poses inside the escape hatch of the *Holland VI*. (Opposite, above) The *Holland VI*, a major breakthrough in submarine design, prepares for its navy trials. (Inset, top) One of Holland's early submarines. (Inset, bottom) The *Plunger*.

The US Navy's **First Submarine**

John Holland had entered three separate design competitions sponsored by the US Navy before finally being awarded a contract in 1895 to build an eighty-five-foot steam-powered submarine, to be called the *Plunger*. Holland was not entirely happy with the navy's demand for the inclusion of a steam engine, and his worst fears proved correct. At the *Plunger*'s launch in 1897, the steam created such heat in the submarine that its crew could not stay inside the vessel. The following March, Holland demonstrated to the navy a gasoline-powered boat he had also developed, the *Holland VI*. In April 1900, after exhaustive trials, the US Navy purchased the *Holland VI* for $150,000 and changed its name to the USS *Holland*. It became the first US Navy submarine.

The Recovery of **Holland 1**

By 1900, Britain's Royal Navy could no longer ignore this "damned un-English weapon." With great secrecy, it ordered the construction of five submarines based on a design licensed from John Holland. With the launch of the first submarine, *Holland 1*, in 1903 (above), the Royal Navy entered the submarine age. *Holland 1* sank in 1913 while under tow in Plymouth Sound. The wreck was discovered in 1981 and raised the following November. It is now on display at the Royal Navy Submarine Museum at Gosport.

(Opposite) The recovered *Holland 1*. (Below) The submarine after salvage. From left to right: in the floating dock; the interior, showing torpedo tube; the propeller; the interior, looking aft.

Chapter Four: **Battle under the Sea**

Germany's fledgling U-boats quickly established themselves as the navy's most effective weapon. Navy artist Claus Bergen depicted their exploits in a series of now-famous paintings, including the one at left. (Right) A German propaganda poster.

First Watch Officer Johannes Spiess called down to his commander, Lieutenant Otto Weddigen of the German submarine *U-9*, who was enjoying his breakfast below. There was something he should see.

When Weddigen peered for himself through his boat's periscope, he could make out three British cruisers, *Aboukir*, *Cressy* and *Hogue* — older ships, but large ones, each displacing some twelve thousand tons. They were steaming slowly off the coast of Holland, in line and making no attempt to zigzag, as if they were on a Sunday afternoon cruise in peacetime. And no escorts were in sight. Weddigen could scarcely believe his good luck. He immediately ordered his crew to stand by for action.

Because of the submarine's slow speed when submerged, it took the U-boat commander more than half an hour to position himself for attack. But at last he had a British cruiser in his sights. At a range of about five hundred yards, he fired a single torpedo at the *Aboukir*. The time was 6:20 A.M. Thirty seconds later, a huge explosion seemed to jar the very ocean. The old cruiser staggered like an elephant hit by a howitzer. She began to settle stern first. The crewmen aboard the *U-9* raised a ragged cheer.

Weddigen's eyes widened as he scanned the scene through the periscope. The second cruiser, *Hogue*, was closing. Not to chase after *U-9*, but to assist in picking up the *Aboukir*'s survivors. Then something astonishing occurred to Weddigen. The British crewmen had not spotted *U-9*'s periscope! They probably thought the cruiser had hit a mine. At 6:55 A.M., Weddigen fired two more torpedoes from about three hundred yards at *Hogue*. Both found their mark. The ship seemed to wince as the torpedoes exploded. In minutes, the sea became a nightmare of desperate men, oil and coal dust.

"Those of us in the conning tower," Spiess later recalled, "tried, by cursing the English, who had incited the Japanese and all Europe against us, to dispel the gruesome impression made on us by the drowning men struggling in the midst of floating wreckage and clinging to the upturned lifeboats."

Twelve minutes later, the third cruiser, *Cressy*, steamed into range as she arrived to assist in the rescue work. Weddigen hardly dared credit the evidence before his eyes. Two cruisers down and still the British hadn't spotted him! It was impossible. Weddigen had already accomplished far more than he could have hoped for. He had every reason to slip away as rapidly as possible. His batteries were almost exhausted and, heaven knows, there might be powerful escorts racing to the scene at that very moment.

But he still had three torpedoes left. And he knew that if he didn't try to sink the *Cressy*, he would regret it for the rest of his life — however long that might be. Without further thought, he turned to attack, firing two of his remaining torpedoes. Both hit the target with awesome impact.

Spiess later remembered the scene: "The giant with four funnels turned slowly to port. Men climbed like ants over her side and then, as she turned turtle completely, they ran about on her broad flat keel until, in a few minutes, she disappeared beneath the waves." He watched it all through the periscope, simultaneously elated and saddened. In a matter of minutes, fourteen hundred men had died, more than had been lost at the Battle of Trafalgar. It was Britain's worst naval humiliation in over a hundred years. And it had been inflicted by a "paraffin-guzzling, flame-belching, smoke-wreathed boat with a crew of twenty-six." The date was September 22, 1914. Britain and Germany had been at war for just seven weeks.

"Those of us in the conning tower tried, by cursing the English…to dispel the gruesome impression made on us by the drowning men struggling in the midst of floating wreckage and clinging to the upturned lifeboats."

— First Watch Officer Johannes Spiess

(Above) The *U-9* off the Hook of Holland, where the three British cruisers were sunk. (Opposite) In Germany, newspapers applauded the attack as an outstanding, heroic deed. Otto Weddigen (right) and all of his crew (far right) were honored with Iron Crosses.

A Deadly **Menace**

Only seven weeks before the *U-9* fired its first torpedo at the *Aboukir*, Germany had sent out ten U-boats on the first submarine war patrol in history. Commander of U-boats Hermann Bauer was confident that the submarines had enormous offensive potential — and the *U-9*'s successful attack on the British cruisers proved it. The U-boats also provided the perfect weapon for fighting the blockade war against Britain. The submarine, by its very nature, could patrol the waters of the North Atlantic unseen — ready to ambush unsuspecting merchant ships heading for English ports with valuable supplies. The faint wake of its all-seeing periscope was the only indication of its deadly presence under the sea.

(Far left and opposite, left) U-boats on the prowl. (Opposite, right) U-boats take on arms and supplies. (Below) A cutaway of the *U-9*. (Left) A German propaganda poster.

Illustrirte Zeitung

Unsere U-Boote

Periscopes

Air compressors

Torpedo loading hatch / escape hatch

Air intake

Aft torpedo tube

Electric motors

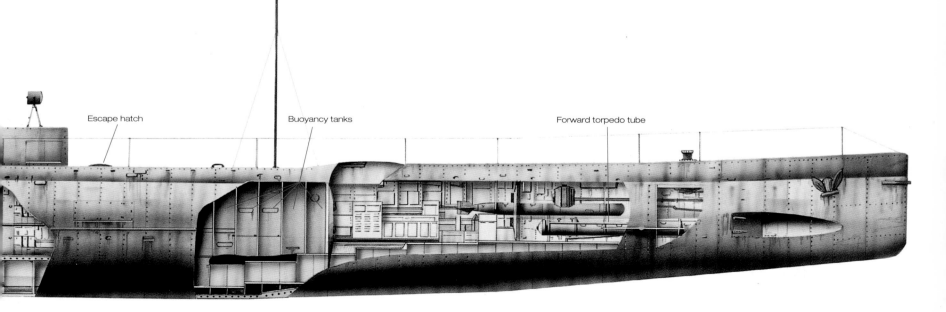

Escape hatch   Buoyancy tanks   Forward torpedo tube

A Powerful Weapon **Unleashed**

Once the U-boat spotted a target, it would unleash one of its powerful self-propelled torpedoes (below) — set to hit the target's unprotected and vulnerable bottom, where its warhead would do the most damage. Firing the torpedo, however, involved more than simply issuing the command to the control room. The U-boat had to maneuver into position first, taking into account the speed of the target and the angle relative to the submarine. Once the weapon was activated, the torpedo's motor ❶ started, driven by compressed air ❷, the propellers ❸ began to turn, and the safety mechanism protecting the detonator began to unwind ❹, arming the warhead ❺.

(Above, right) Lookouts on the conning tower of a U-boat scan the seas for enemy ships. (Left) Readying for attack, crewmembers charge the sub's torpedo tubes. (Above, left) Tension mounts in the control room as a U-boat descends for cover after being spotted by an Allied vessel.

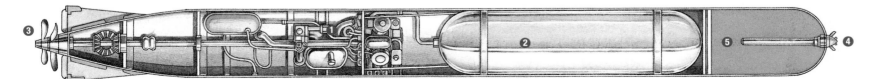

(Below) A German propaganda poster for the blockade against Britain. As Germany escalated its attacks against ships in the North Atlantic, ads in New York newspapers (bottom) warned Americans of the dangers of crossing the ocean.

More shocks followed the loss of the three British cruisers. Less than a month later, Germany's *U-17* encountered the 866-ton British merchant ship *Glitra* off the coast of Norway. The luckless *Glitra* was soon diving helplessly to the seabed. But not thanks to a torpedo. Following the so-called Prize Rules dating back to the era of Napoleon, *U-17*'s sailors had boarded her and, after verifying that her cargo was indeed contraband, had opened her seacocks. She was the first merchant ship ever sunk by a submarine — the first of some five thousand that would be lost in the Great War. While the Royal Navy worried about Germany's dreadnoughts, a new and potent force was coming into being: a handful of deadly U-boats lurking in the unfriendly waters of the North Sea.

On New Year's Day, 1915, the same *U-17* delivered a sad postscript to the story of the *Aboukir*, *Cressy* and *Hogue*. She torpedoed the battleship HMS *Formidable*, killing more than half of the crew of eight hundred. Although other vessels were in the area, none came near to offer help. The navy had strictly forbidden any of its ships to go to the aid of others in sub-infested waters.

The submarine's possibilities, already shown in a few isolated cases to be frighteningly effective, were about to be displayed in an even more alarming and widespread fashion.

In November 1914, Great Britain had declared the entire North Sea a war zone. This gave the Royal Navy the right to stop, board, search and detain any vessel found in these waters — a move that effectively killed Germany's international trade.

Early in 1915, Germany retaliated by declaring the waters around the British Isles a war zone. Any ship found there after February 18 was liable to be attacked without warning. Then the submarines of the German High Seas Fleet headed for British waters.

On May 1, 1915, the RMS *Lusitania* set sail from New York for Liverpool. Days before the great Cunarder's departure, ads had appeared in the New York papers warning would-be transatlantic passengers that British ships were "liable to destruction." Although these notices were attributed to the Imperial German Embassy, they had been paid for by German-American businessmen who were growing uneasy about the deteriorating relationship between Germany and the United States. Despite the warnings, the Cunard line received few cancellations. This early in the war, few people believed that anyone would attack a passenger ship.

The same day, the American tanker *Gulflight* was damaged by a U-boat's torpedo, apparently a case of mistaken identity. Although three Americans were killed and the press voiced outrage, President Woodrow Wilson took no action. He had correctly judged the American people's mood.

Germany must be made aware that it had overstepped the bounds of civilized conduct, but few Americans wanted to go to war over the incident.

On Friday, May 7, as the *Lusitania* neared the end of her voyage, *U-20*, under the command of Lieutenant Walther Schweiger, surfaced shortly after noon and spotted the big liner. The Irish coast was visible, a thin dark line ten miles distant.

William Turner, *Lusitania*'s captain, was steering his vessel close to Brow Head, Galley Head and the Old Head of Kinsale. He knew the coast well; he had sailed this way dozens of times before. He also knew that the Admiralty had warned merchant ships to stay away from the headlands — where U-boats tended to lurk — and to sail in the middle of the sea lane, which meant about seventy miles offshore. But Turner wasn't worried. He was fond of telling anyone within earshot that the *Lusitania* could outrun any submarine. The big liner was making about eighteen knots as she approached Queenstown (later renamed Cobh). And her course was undeviating in perfectly calm conditions. It was not that Turner dismissed the Admiralty's instructions out of hand. It was a matter of interpretation. The navy's business was to defeat the enemy. His was to get his passengers to port as speedily and as comfortably as possible. Many of those aboard the *Lusitania* had paid more for their passages than most mortals earned in a year. They expected a smooth passage, and Captain Turner intended to provide it.

A deckhand named Leslie Morton spotted the torpedo from his watch position on the starboard bow. He grabbed his megaphone.

"Torpedo coming on the starboard side!"

At precisely 2:10 P.M., the missile with its three-hundred-pound charge struck the huge liner. A booming explosion echoed across the tranquil sea. A second, louder, explosion occurred a moment later — almost certainly the result of coal dust igniting in the ship's bunkers. The massive vessel began to list. Eighteen minutes after Schwieger's torpedo struck her, the *Lusitania* disappeared into the dark Atlantic, taking 1,195 passengers with her — including 123 Americans.

News of the sinking shocked the world. In Britain and America, it elbowed every other story off the front pages. How, people asked themselves, could a civilized nation commit such a despicable act? Newspapers outdid each other in their indignation. New York howled about the Germans making war "like savages drunk with blood." London called the sinking "a dastardly, piratical act" and "the foulest of the many foul crimes that have stained German arms." Particularly galling was the fact that the famous liner had been torpedoed without warning.

Berlin apologized to the United States, expressing its "deepest sympathy" at the loss of American lives — but pointed out that the responsibility for the tragedy rested with the British government which, "through its plan of starving the civilian population," had forced Germany into taking retaliatory measures.

Trapped on the Lusitania

In August 1993, underwater explorer Dr. Robert Ballard led an expedition to the wreck of the *Lusitania* off the coast of Ireland. Using the minisubmarine *Delta* and remotely controlled camera vehicles, Ballard and his team studied and photographed the wreck in hopes of discovering clues to the cause of the second explosion that occurred after the liner was torpedoed. Marine artist Ken Marschall, famous for his haunting paintings of the *Titanic*, accompanied Ballard on the expedition and made several trips in the *Delta* to study the wreck firsthand. During one of these trips — with historian Eric Sauder also aboard — the minisub's stern propeller became snagged in the fishing nets that cling to the *Lusitania* (right). Luckily, the rear rudder and propeller could be jettisoned, and the minisub floated free. (Far right) Marschall's painting of the *Lusitania* on the ocean floor.

Soon after the sinking of the *Lusitania*, both Britain and Germany began viewing the U-boat campaign with growing concern — but each for very different reasons. The British worried about the loss of merchant ships to U-boats and feared that perhaps the seemingly unstoppable underwater craft could cost them the war. Paradoxically, the very success of the campaign troubled the Germans. They now realized that if the sinkings continued, the Americans — with their wealth, manpower and industrial capacity — would inevitably be drawn into the war on the Allied side.

In August 1915, the White Star liner *Arabic* was torpedoed, with the loss of forty-four passengers and crew — three of them American citizens. This time, President Wilson protested strongly. Although some senior German officers still supported the unrestricted U-boat warfare, cooler heads prevailed. U-boat captains were ordered not to attack any more passenger ships.

Sinkings declined and on September 20, 1915, most of the U-boats in British waters withdrew. The first campaign had lasted over seven months. By the end of that year, Britain had lost a staggering 855,000 tons of shipping to submarine attacks; Germany, a mere twenty U-boats. Mines, most of them sown by the small submarines designed for this work, accounted for the loss of a further ninety-four ships.

A German Sub Arrives in **America**

In July 1916, as the U-boat offensive continued in the Atlantic, the unarmed German merchant submarine *Deutschland* (left) arrived in Baltimore, Maryland, on the first of two "friendly" trips to the United States. The cargo-carrying freighter was the first submarine to be used for non-military purposes — and it was also the first to make a transatlantic crossing. She returned to Germany with her holds full of tin, nickel and rubber — all purchased legally in neutral America. After the US entered the war in April 1917, she was converted into a long-distance U-cruiser.

Germany's Unrestricted **U-boat Campaign**

Throughout the war, Germany launched several brutal and unrestricted U-boat campaigns that succeeded in crippling Allied shipping in the North Atlantic. The first one, put into operation shortly after the Kaiser declared the waters around Britain a war zone, lasted until September 1915 — when Germany bowed to the mounting public outrage at the increasingly coldblooded tactics used by the U-boats, particularly after the sinking of the *Lusitania*. The lull was short-lived, however, and in March 1916, the U-boats resumed their carnage on the high seas. In February 1917, after the final and most aggressive U-boat campaign was unleashed, the situation for Britain quickly became dire. One out of every four merchant ships leaving its ports was lost. It was only after the United States entered the war in April 1917, bringing with it enormous industrial support for Britain, that the beleaguered island found the resolve to fight back with what would prove to be its most effective anti-U-boat weapon — the convoy.

Despite the staggering losses suffered, the Allies had not yet done much to develop any effective antisubmarine weapons. Cash inducements by the British Admiralty for firm sightings of U-boats had accomplished little. Very few small vessels carried radio; if they spotted a U-boat, they could not report the sighting until they returned to port — and by then it was inevitably too late. The French had fared a little better. An engineer named Paul Langevin made some progress with an underwater echo-ranging device. In Britain, a former destroyer captain named C.P. Ryan developed hydrophones in an effort to detect U-boats beneath the surface. Although they were used on ASW

Desperate to counter the heavy losses inflicted by U-boats, the British Navy put into operation an array of antisubmarine devices — including hydrophones (top) and the decoy Q-ships (above). (Opposite) A U-boat searches for merchant ships in the North Atlantic.

(antisubmarine warfare) picket boats as early as 1915, the equipment was not sophisticated enough to establish the position of a submarine — only its presence in the water.

Another French invention was the so-called "sound lenses," a pair of bulges in the hull positioned close to a ship's bow, each with a fly's-eye pattern of diaphragms and ear trumpets. The diaphragms recording the strongest vibrations would be at right angles to the source. The device was tried, but eventually rejected as too fragile for service use.

Among Britain's most colorful antisubmarine weapons were the famous "Q-ships." To the casual observer, they were nondescript merchant ships, trawlers or tramps. In fact, they were well armed with torpedoes and guns — but the weapons were craftily concealed. Lifeboats were sliced in half at the waist so they could be pulled apart quickly to uncover a gun station. Dummy deckhouses had hinged walls. At night, the crews were kept busy adding dummy funnels or repainting the ship. And although the Q-ships were manned by the Royal Navy, the crews affected a slovenliness, in keeping with their undercover work. If the disguises were ingenious, it was because they had to be. Many U-boat captains were former merchant sailors familiar with the decks and crews of tramp steamers.

The tricky decision for a Q-ship skipper was exactly when to drop his ship's disguise. The nearer he could get to his prey, the more likely his chances of destroying it. At the same time, the longer he delayed, the fiercer the gunfire that might come his way at any moment.

About 180 vessels were converted to Q-ships. They sank only fourteen U-boats, but they damaged many more, some seriously. At the time, so much secrecy surrounded the Q-ships that few people knew anything about them. Subsequently, they received a good deal of attention but they were never a particularly effective antisubmarine weapon. U-boat captains became understandably cautious when approaching tramps and merchantmen, only too aware of what might happen. And they took to torpedoing them while safely submerged, often with great loss of life. Q-ships were phased out when convoys became widespread in mid-1917.

Patrols by aircraft would have been the most efficient means of combating U-boats. Unfortunately, the aircraft of the day didn't have the necessary range, nor did they have any means of dropping weapons accurately. The crews simply slung small bombs over the side or dropped them from wing racks and hoped for the best. Blimps were useful at spotting U-boats, although their modest speed limited their usefulness in attack. The navy tended to favor the use of fast destroyers and patrol boats.

Civilians also had plenty of ideas on how to deal with U-boats. Most were wildly impractical. One man recommended enormous magnets to drag the boats down to the ocean floor and keep them there. Another suggested trained seagulls that would gather over submerged submarines, marking the targets for the antisubmarine forces. Unfortunately, the enthusiastic inventor had no idea how the gulls were to be trained!

In 1915, aware of the urgent need to counter U-boat attacks, the Admiralty had turned to an idea suggested by Sir Charles Madden, a Grand Fleet staff officer — a mine that exploded when it sank to a preset depth. The depth charge combined some three hundred pounds of high explosive with a pressure-sensitive firing mechanism to create an effective anti-U-boat weapon — although it was not until the spring of 1916 that these were available in any numbers. Initially rolled off racks at the stern of destroyers or other speedy vessels, the depth charges were soon being "thrown" by special equipment that could hurl the devices about seventy-five feet — much like an army mortar.

Sea mines, laid in great fields around Britain's coast to target German surface ships, also helped in the fight against the U-boat. But by far, the most effective antisubmarine weapon was the convoy — an idea borrowed from the Royal Navy of the Napoleonic era and introduced in the spring of 1917, shortly after the United States entered the war. Soon, destroyers and other naval vessels were shepherding large numbers of merchant ships across the Atlantic with relatively few losses.

By the summer of 1918, the U-boats were suffering insupportable casualties. The U-boat flotilla in Flanders, for example, was losing one boat per week. Maintenance and repairs were cut to a minimum in order to keep sizeable numbers of the underwater craft in action. But despite the weakened state of its U-boat fleet, Germany still had one ace up its sleeve — the U-cruisers, which came into being in 1917. With a displacement of some twenty-five hundred tons, these formidable vessels were the largest submarines built during the First World War. One of the first U-cruisers, *U-155*, set off on patrol from Kiel in May 1917. She sailed more than ten thousand miles, sank nineteen ships, and

(Above) A page from the British magazine *The Sphere* depicts how Allied merchant ships could avoid attacks by U-boats. (Opposite) Three flying boats bomb a German submarine in a watercolor by C.R. Fleming-Williams. (Right) A British sailor stands ready to catapult a depth charge into the air.

Black Sunday in American Waters

With the addition of long-distance undersea-cruisers to its U-boat fleet in mid-1917, Germany could expand its aggressive Atlantic campaign to the North American coast. In early May 1918, U-cruiser *U-151* arrived off the US northeast coast. During a destructive nine-week assault, it attacked and disabled twenty-three ships by gunfire, bombs or torpedoes — all without a single loss of life. Its most infamous tally, however, came on June 2. On that day alone, immortalized as Black Sunday, *U-151* destroyed six American vessels — among them, the passenger liner SS *Carolina*, en route to New York from San Juan, Puerto Rico, with 217 passengers and 113 crew on board. Although the German U-boat had observed Prize Rules and set the officers, men, women and children adrift at sea before it shelled the unlucky liner, not everyone made it safely to shore. During a fierce storm the first night, thirteen passengers — including two women — drowned when the ship's motor launch foundered and overturned.

(Above) The SS *Carolina*. (Left) Grim-faced survivors pose in borrowed clothes forty-eight hours after they made it safely to shore at Atlantic City, New Jersey. (Top) The *Carolina* sinking became a rallying cry for Americans to support the war effort in Europe. (Below) The *U-151*.

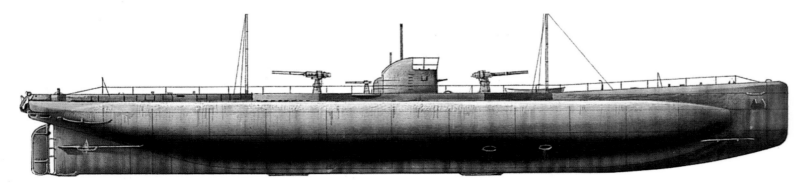

shelled the Azores. Another U-cruiser, *U-151*, traveled more than twelve thousand miles and sank thirteen ships. Her successes encouraged the Germans to send more of the hefty U-cruisers across the Atlantic. But the great days of Germany's submarine might were dwindling rapidly.

By the autumn of 1918, the first major undersea war was almost over. Rumors of mutiny and revolution infected every level of German society. By early November, most German battleships were flying the revolutionary red flag. Orders given to U-boats to torpedo such ships only added to the chaos. The disciplined German state had disintegrated; confusion and upheaval were everywhere. The ferment spread to major cities. The population was utterly exhausted from the effort of trying to win a war against the now-overwhelming might of her enemies. A general strike paralyzed an already tottering economy. The Kaiser abdicated.

The U-boat fleet, still unbeaten by the enemy, was loyal and disciplined to the last. It was ordered by the British Admiralty to the port of Harwich on England's east coast. There, Royal Navy warships marshaled the U-boats and British crews took them over, hoisting the White Ensign above the German flag and stripping the captive boats of any offensive equipment. In all, 176 U-boats entered captivity; 226 more were found at Krupp and other yards, still under construction — intended for a mighty U-boat offensive that never took place.

Germany had started the war with 28 operational U-boats and had built another 344. One hundred and seventy-eight had been lost in action. Thirteen thousand officers and men had served on the U-boats; of these, nearly five thousand lost their lives during the war. But if the U-boats' losses were grievous, the losses inflicted on the Allies were also staggering. Five thousand ships had gone down to the U-boats, totaling an incredible twelve million tons of shipping, most of it British. The U-boats had killed more than fifteen thousand British seamen and had come close to winning the war for Germany. Ironically, the very success of Germany's submarine war had virtually guaranteed involvement by the United States — and that, in turn, ensured the defeat of the Central Powers.

When peace was restored, the Treaty of Versailles decreed that the entire U-boat fleet be scrapped. Germany must never again be allowed to claim supremacy on the high seas. In fact, one British newspaper angrily demanded that the Kaiser and all U-boat commanders be hanged without delay. In the shadow of his country's defeat, one German prisoner of war, twenty-seven-year-old Karl Dönitz, was already dreaming of a restored U-boat fleet — and the next battle under the sea.

He would not have to dream long.

After the Armistice was signed in November 1918, all operational U-boats were handed over to the British and interned at Harwich, on England's east coast. By the following April, all had been dispersed among the Allies or used for tests and later scrapped.

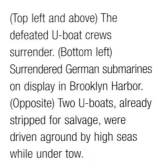

(Top left and above) The defeated U-boat crews surrender. (Bottom left) Surrendered German submarines on display in Brooklyn Harbor. (Opposite) Two U-boats, already stripped for salvage, were driven aground by high seas while under tow.

AE2 — A Hero of Gallipoli

One of the most daring submarine feats of World War I made headlines again in 1998, when the wreck of the Royal Australian Navy submarine *AE2* was discovered at the bottom of the Sea of Marmara. In April of 1915, this E-class sub was ordered to attempt the near-impossible — breach the narrow, heavily mined Dardanelles Strait and "generally run amuck — if you get there." The mission was part of a disastrous campaign championed by Winston Churchill, then Britain's First Lord of the Admiralty, to send warships through the impenetrable Dardanelles, land Allied troops at Gallipoli and knock Germany's ally, Turkey, out of the war.

Two submarines had already tried — and failed — to negotiate the narrow forty-mile strait. In fact, no enemy craft in five hundred years had successfully made it through the Dardanelles. But early on the morning of April 25, 1915 — the same day that troops landed on the beaches at Gallipoli — the *AE2* slipped into the treacherous passage. After scraping against mines, beaching itself twice right beneath Turkish fortifications and evading enemy tows that tried to grapple the sub, the *AE2* entered the Sea of Marmara on April 26.

The Australian submarine's astonishing success was welcome news to the battered Allies on shore. British commander Sir Ian Hamilton, who had been considering withdrawal, issued his famous "dig, dig, dig yourselves in and stick it out" order to his forces — made up mainly of Australians and New Zealanders. (It is claimed that the term "Digger" was thus coined for the ANZAC troops.)

But *AE2*'s luck quickly ran out. On April 30, she surfaced near a Turkish gunboat, which holed her hull with three shells. Unable to dive, Commander Henry Stoker surrendered his crew (left), then scuttled the sub. He and his thirty-one men spent the rest of the war in captivity. Allied troops were not evacuated until eight months after the *AE2*'s sinking — by which time casualties on both sides exceeded 250,000.

H.M.A SUBMARINE "AE2" AT PORTSMOUTH. FEB.1914.
OFFICERS AND CREW @ FORT BLOCKHOUSE @

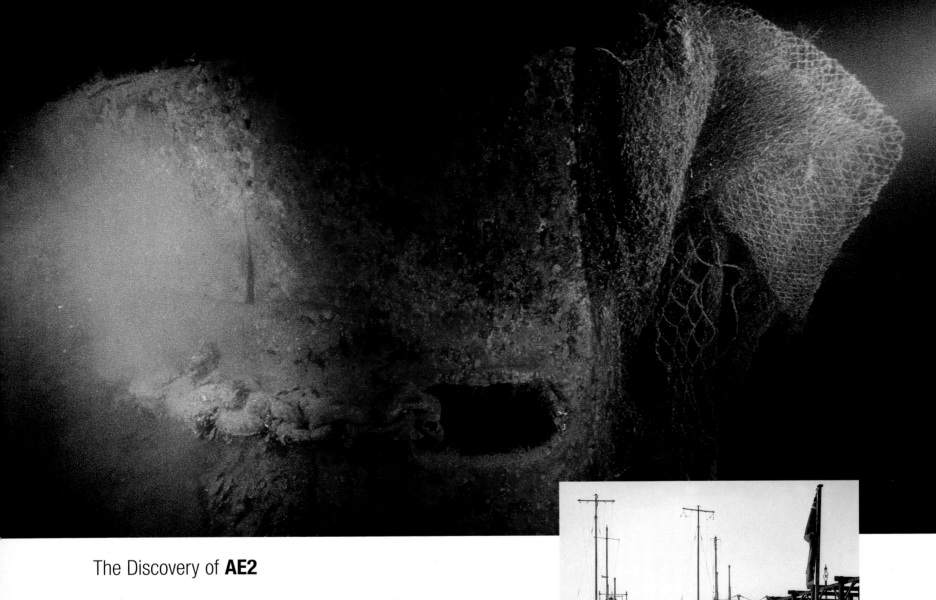

The Discovery of **AE2**

Intrigued by the daring exploits of the *AE2*, Turkish underwater explorer and museum director Selçuk Kolay initiated a search for the submarine in 1996. Using sophisticated sonar and magnetometric equipment, Kolay finally located the wreck of the *AE2* in June 1998. A joint Australian-Turkish expedition of divers and archaeologists, led by Australian Dr. Mark Spencer, has explored and documented the submarine several times since. The wreck is remarkably intact, and efforts are now underway to continue the crucial archaeological monitoring of the site before deciding whether the *AE2* might eventually be raised.

(Top) John Thomson, left, grandson of Leading Seaman Thomson of the *AE2*, assists Dr. Mark Spencer before a dive on the wreck site. (Above) Dr. Spencer, left, and Selçuk Kolay exchange congratulations during one of the first expeditions to the *AE2*. (Opposite) A shroud of fishing nets covers the rusted bow of the Australian submarine. (Inset) The *AE2* in port at Sydney, New South Wales, in 1914. (Right) An expedition diver swims over the sub's stern casing (top) and holds one of the propeller blades (bottom).

Chapter Five: **Lost in Peace**

Despite advancements in submarine technology after the First World War, crewmembers had no way of escaping from a sunken submarine until 1927, when now-standard rescue equipment was first developed — including the Davis Submerged Escape Apparatus (opposite), the Momsen Lung and the McCann Rescue Chamber.

In the twenties and early thirties, the world's navies — held back in part by restrictive treaties — added relatively few submarines to their fleets. Those that were built, however, more than made up in size what they lacked in numbers. Britain built the giant *X-1*, an experimental ocean raider inspired by the German cruiser submarines. As well, Britain's new M-class submarines — completed in the dying days of the First World War — boasted twelve-inch guns, weapons better suited to a battleship than a submersible. One of the class, *M-2*, later traded her big gun for a hangar and scout-plane catapult. The French added the mighty *Surcouf* to their fleet in 1929. Nearly 360 feet long, she was for many years the world's largest submarine — an honor she would not surrender until the eve of the Second World War.

As the thirties wore on, the possibility of another war seemed ever more likely. Germany secretly resumed building U-boats after Hitler took power, and the Japanese and the Italians also went to work on their fleets. Fearing what was to come — and with the lessons of the First World War still fresh in their minds — the United States and Britain began building large numbers of patrol submarines, which they hoped would give them the edge in any future underwater battles.

Two submarine disasters dominated newspaper headlines during this time. Both involved modern boats, early examples of classes that would go on to have distinguished wartime records. And both boasted the latest in safety equipment. That they sank in peacetime was a grim reminder of how dangerous submarines still were — especially for their crews.

On May 23, 1939, USS *Squalus* left the picturesque town of Portsmouth, New Hampshire, to carry out a dive as part of its acceptance trials. The latest in fleet-type submarines, the *Squalus* was 308 feet long, 27 feet wide, with a surface displacement of 1,450 tons. Her propulsion was diesel-electric, and her twin 1,400 HP electric motors could drive her at twenty knots on the surface and around nine knots submerged. With a crew of four officers and fifty-one men under the command of thirty-four-year-old Lieutenant Oliver Naquin of New Orleans, she was scheduled to make her nineteenth test dive — an emergency battle descent plunging to fifty feet in sixty seconds.

Three civilian technicians were also on board as the *Squalus* headed for a point thirteen miles from Portsmouth, near White Island. There, Naquin gave the order "Rig for dive."

Not long afterward, Portsmouth received a radio message from the *Squalus* advising that the submarine would be diving at longitude 70 degrees, 31 minutes west. But a radioman had recorded the message incorrectly; the submarine's actual position was 70 degrees, 36 minutes west.

Bristling with heavy guns, Britain's *M-1* (above) was the first of a new generation of submarines designed especially for war.

(Right) The USS *Squalus* in January 1938 during construction at the Portsmouth Navy Yard. This view, looking aft, shows a cross section of the pressure hull and main ballast tanks. (Far right) By April, the bows were taking shape around the forward torpedo tube. (Below) The submarine was launched on September 14, 1938. Its number was changed to SS 192 prior to commissioning.

"I felt a sudden terrific increase in pressure and…I was struck on the back with a volume of water coming in the ventilation line directly over me, driving my head and shoulders down…. Water was flowing through the door…. Emergency lights went out."

— *Squalus* survivor and naval architect
Harold C. Preble

(Opposite) Artist John Groth vividly re-creates the drama in the control room of the *Squalus*. Moments after the stricken submarine hit the ocean bottom, crewmen frantically struggled to close off water leaks as the impact of the descent flung them against one another and onto the floor. (Above) The USS *Sculpin*.

At 8:35 A.M., Naquin gave the order "Stand by to dive!" Five minutes later, the first blast of the diving alarm started the dive. The diesels were stopped; the forward main ballast tanks were flooded. The main motors were still driving the boat at sixteen knots. In the control room, the heart of the submarine — where a dazzling array of dials, lights and levers controlled and monitored every function of the boat — the diving officer surveyed the control board, or "Christmas Tree." This consisted of rows of red and green lights, each representing a specific hull aperture. Red meant "open." Green meant "closed." A glance at the board indicated all green. As Naquin nodded his assent, the diving officer sounded the second blast of the alarm and flooded the remaining ballast tanks.

It took the submarine precisely sixty-two seconds to reach a depth of fifty feet. Everything appeared to be operating correctly when an ominous message was relayed to Control over the telephone: "Flooding in the after engine room." The water was cascading in amid the machinery and electrical circuits that gave the vessel life. And still the Christmas Tree indicated all green.

The diving officer ordered all ballast, emergency and forward buoyancy tanks blown. The boat began to level off — and then it suddenly sank by the stern. Too much water had already poured into the submarine, and the enormous weight of the flooded compartments dragged the vessel down. She settled on the seabed, in total darkness 243 feet below the surface.

Naquin had little doubt about the cause. Earlier tests had raised questions about the main induction valve in the top of the bridge structure which supplied the diesel engines with air. This was where the water was entering. Already the rear compartments were flooded, eradicating any hope for the men there.

Fortuitously, *Squalus*'s sister ship, the *Sculpin*, was about to depart on a two-month shakedown cruise to South America. Rear Admiral Cyrus W. Cole, commanding the Portsmouth Navy Yard, ordered the *Sculpin* to sail to the point from which the *Squalus* had dived and to initiate a search. She arrived at 1 P.M., nearly five hours after the fatal dive — but, because of the error in transmission, some five miles east of the *Squalus*'s actual position. By the greatest of good fortune, however, a young ensign named Ned Denby, on watch on the *Sculpin*'s bridge, caught a glimpse of something on the horizon. It *might* have been a distress signal flare. Fifteen minutes later, Ensign Denby spotted the sixth flare the trapped crew had fired.

Then another flare exploded, almost directly in front of the *Sculpin*. Moments later, lookouts spotted a marker buoy bobbing in the restless sea and hauled it onto the *Sculpin*'s deck with boat hooks. The buoy had a long telephone line attached to it, and contact was established between the

Charles B. **Momsen**

(Right) Charles Momsen demonstrates his lifesaving Submarine Escape Lung, a portable breathing apparatus that enabled trapped crewmen to exit a stricken submarine. The oblong rubber bag contained a canister of soda lime, which removed poisonous carbon dioxide from the air and then replenished the air with oxygen. The Momsen Lung also allowed a submariner to rise slowly to the surface, preventing the onset of "the bends." (Above) Momsen with the decompression chamber he helped develop.

captains of the two submarines — but only for a few seconds. The *Sculpin* rose suddenly, carried by a boisterous wave, and the line went dead.

Luckily, the correct position of the submarine was now known, and more help was on the way. A converted World War I minesweeper, USS *Falcon*, had been dispatched from Portsmouth with the most recent addition to the Navy's submarine rescue equipment — a ten-ton diving bell, officially known as the McCann Rescue Chamber. Ten feet high and seven feet wide, the pear-shaped steel rescue device was divided internally into upper and lower compartments. Raised and lowered by ballast tanks, and guided along a four-hundred-foot length of half-inch steel wire, it attached snugly to the hatch of a damaged submarine, thanks to a rubber collar around its base. It could accommodate seven survivors at a time. Although the McCann Rescue Chamber was superior to any rescue device in existence at the time, it was still in the experimental stages. This would be its first real test.

Coincidentally, the inventor of the chamber, Lieutenant Commander Charles B. Momsen, was at that moment aboard a twin-engined amphibian headed for the site of the sinking. The forty-three-year-old Momsen had dedicated much of his career to the saving of submariners' lives. He is probably most famous for the invention of the Momsen Lung, a portable escape gear that was carried aboard the *Squalus*. Momsen also developed a rescue chamber while at the navy's Bureau of Construction and Repair. After his transfer, his invention was further refined by his successor, Lieutenant Commander Allan R. McCann, for whom it was named.

A number of reporters had already converged on the scene in small boats that bobbed about in the choppy water; overhead, light aircraft circled expectantly. The fate of the *Squalus* and her crew was rapidly becoming the biggest story of the day. All America, it seemed, was praying for the

(Below) As rescue efforts proceeded above, the thirty-three *Squalus* survivors huddled in the cold and darkness below, trying to keep warm.

submariners. And good luck had already had a hand. Soon, Momsen and the chamber would be on site. If, for any reason, the chamber couldn't be used, the Momsen Lung would have to be employed —but this was a much riskier method, in view of the depth involved. Even the most experienced diver ran the risk of nitrogen poisoning — the insidious "bends" — when working so far below the surface. (Coincidentally, Momsen had been experimenting for several months with a helium-oxygen mixture in his breathing apparatus, which would have extended its range to a depth of three hundred feet. It was not yet ready.)

(Below) The rescue ships USS *Falcon,* right, and USS *Wandank,* left, on site over the sunken *Squalus.* The McCann Rescue Chamber (visible on the *Falcon*'s afterdeck, below) is readied (far left) for lowering overboard (left, top). This was its inaugural rescue mission. (Left, bottom) Lieutenant Commander Allan R. McCann, left, during initial testing of the rescue chamber at the Brooklyn Navy Yard in the early thirties.

In the submarine, the survivors were well but cold. Pressure was about 12.5 pounds above atmospheric and therefore not harmful to the crew. Portable battery-powered lamps were being used for light.

The weather was beginning to deteriorate when the *Falcon* finally arrived on the scene, twenty-three hours after the sinking. The first step was to string the downhaul wire for the rescue chamber from the *Falcon* to the sub. Diver Martin Sibitzky, a boatswain's mate, was fortunate enough to land on the *Squalus* a mere six feet from the forward escape hatch. Sibitzky could hear the hammer blows from the sailors within. He banged the deck in acknowledgment, then busied himself connecting the end of the downhaul wire to the large metal ring in the center of the escape hatch. On the second try, he shackled the wire into the "bail" and prepared to come up.

The next step was to hoist the rescue chamber off the *Falcon*'s fantail. Newscaster Bob Trout witnessed the operation: "We reporters up here really don't know what to call it. Officially it's a rescue chamber, but it sort of looks like a bell. All of us here, however, know that we are witnessing a historic event."

The operators on this first rescue attempt were Walt Harmon and John Mihalowski. For a few moments, the chamber crept along the surface like some monstrous insect. Then it disappeared. At 150 feet, the descent had to be halted momentarily while a minor air-vent problem was fixed. The plunge continued, the chamber sliding easily through the dark water, stopping several times so the crew could make sure the wire was winding correctly on the winch. In a matter of minutes, contact would be made with the imprisoned sailors.

The McCann **Rescue Chamber**

(Right) *The Illustrated London News* spotlighted the key role the chamber played in the successful rescue of all survivors aboard the *Squalus*. (Below) A diagram showing the chamber's pressurized interior and its main components. Attached to the larger, upper compartment were air supply and atmospheric exhaust hoses, as well as electric cables for telephone and lights. A horizontal bulkhead, with a watertight hatch in the middle, separated the two compartments. (Bottom) A diagram showing where the flooding occurred aboard the *Squalus*.

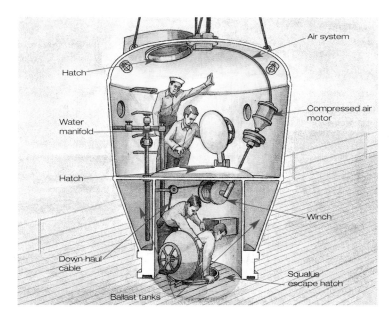

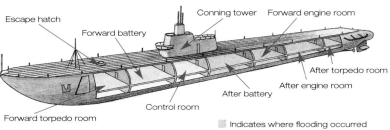

The chamber eased to a halt directly over the hatch. Harmon blew compressed air into the lower chamber, forcing the water out. The crushing pressure of the sea helped to provide a perfect seal between the sub and the chamber. The final step was to attach four bolts that would secure the chamber during the rescue operation. Now came the telling moment. Harmon opened the sub's hatch.

"Hello!" he called. No one replied. For an instant, he felt a surge of panic — then he realized the crew had secured the inner hatch and couldn't hear him.

It was magic when he opened the second hatch. Lights from the rescue bell flooded into the dark, dank interior, revealing a cluster of faces, once drawn and anxious, now alive with hope. The men took great gulps of the deliciously fresh air that flowed into the submarine. Gratefully, they accepted the sandwiches, hot soup, warm blankets and flashlights the rescuers had brought.

But their ordeal wasn't over — not yet. The chamber still had to be hauled to the surface, not once but several times, carrying a few survivors on each trip. Both crews knew how meticulously the operation had to be performed. An error in the ballast, and the chamber might become too buoyant, rise too rapidly and crash into the keel of the *Falcon*. In a matter of seconds, triumph could turn to tragedy.

(Opposite) A survivor emerges from the upper hatch of the rescue chamber. (Above) Blanketed survivors aboard the Coast Guard cutter *Harriet Lane*. (Below) Lieutenant Oliver Naquin, commanding officer of the USS *Squalus*.

Seven men went to the surface on the first trip, a thirty-minute journey that must have seemed endless. Lieutenant J.C. Nichols was the first man out; he appeared haggard and unkempt but otherwise was remarkably well. So were the others as, one by one, they clambered out of the rescue capsule and onto the deck of the *Falcon*. One man fainted briefly, overcome by the delightful air that was so fresh it was intoxicating.

On the next trip, nine men were brought to the surface; nine more followed soon afterward. At last, only Naquin and seven other survivors remained to be rescued.

Once the men were safely inside the rescue chamber, the diving bell began its slow ascent to the surface — only to stall at 160 feet. Reversing the winch didn't help. The wire was jammed on the reel. As the operators heaved on the wire to try to pull it free, it started to pop apart until only a single strand remained. Aboard the *Falcon*, elation gave way to concern. The men would have to be lowered carefully *back* to the ocean floor, to wait there while the existing wire was cut free and a new length attached.

Numbly, the survivors gazed at the depth gauge as the chamber made its laborious way back to the sunken *Squalus*.

Aboard the *Falcon*, Momsen ordered diver Jesse Duncan down to secure a second retrieving cable to the rescue bell. Duncan tried, but the pressure defeated him; almost incoherent, he had to be pulled back to the surface and rushed into the decompression chamber. Another man tried. He, too, was beaten by the pressure, the nitrogen and the grasping fingers of frayed wire that entangled and ripped at his suit. He, too, was hurriedly brought back to the surface and taken immediately to the decompression chamber.

Now all the choices had come down to one last, desperate one. It would have to be done without cables. By meticulously controlling the ballast, the rescue team could give the chamber just enough buoyancy so that it would rise slowly while the men on the *Falcon* hauled in the frayed wire by hand.

It was a laborious and painstaking task. But it worked. Thirty-nine hours after the *Squalus* sank, the rescue mission was over. The survivors fell into a deep sleep in the decompression chamber; the next morning, they left for Portsmouth and for eventual reunion with their families and friends. Thirty-three men had been rescued; twenty-six perished in the flooding shortly after impact.

Salvaging the **Squalus**

After the last of the survivors had been rescued from the stricken *Squalus* and a search made of the flooded aft section, the decision was immediately made to begin salvage operations. It would prove to be a task far more difficult than anyone imagined. The downed vessel was lying 243 feet below the surface — significantly deeper than any previous navy submarine salvage operation. Luckily, recently introduced helium-oxygen diving equipment allowed divers to work in the greater water depth. Over the course of the three-month operation, 648 dives would be made to the site.

Rear Admiral Cole commanded the salvage unit, and the *Falcon* was again the primary work platform. The plan called for raising the *Squalus* with pontoons and the submarine's own internal buoyancy. However, because of the deep water, it was not possible to determine the exact center of gravity or buoyancy needed to lift the vessel evenly to the surface. With one end rising first, the salvage crew would have to monitor carefully the angle at which the sub was brought to the surface — to prevent any flooding from open bottom ballast tanks. To control the angle, the *Squalus* would be lifted a short distance, towed submerged to shallow water, and lifted again. To limit the distance of each lift, divers arranged the pontoons at different levels between the surface and the submarine. The upper pontoons controlled the height of the lift.

After fifty days spent getting the equipment in position, the first lift was attempted on July 13 — but it ended disastrously. According to Commander Momsen, "the bow came up like a mad tornado, out of control. Pontoons were smashed, hoses cut and I might add hearts were broken." It took another twenty days to rig the equipment for another try. A second lift succeeded in getting the sub to a grounding site in ninety-two feet of water. After several more attempts there to get the *Squalus* free, she was finally lifted successfully (opposite) and dry-docked at Portsmouth on September 13, 1939.

(Left) A diagram depicts the positioning of the salvage pontoons. In mid-August, the *Squalus* was finally brought to within 92 feet of the surface. (Above) After the pontoons were blown (far left), they rose, churning the water as they carried the weight of the submarine upward (middle left). The control pontoons float on the water (middle right) as a tug tows the *Squalus*, now suspended below the surface by pontoons. (Far right) In late August, the unwieldy submarine was not yet raised. (Below) A tense moment aboard the *Falcon*.

Diagram labels:
USS *Falcon*
Distance sub would rise until control pontoons reach surface
Air hoses to pump out ballast and fuel tanks
Control pontoons
Squalus 243' below surface, at 11° tilt

The men aboard the Royal Navy's *Thetis* were not as lucky as the men on the *Squalus*. The *Thetis* was one of Britain's new T-class submarines; these vessels, with their ten twenty-one-inch torpedo tubes, were among the most formidable in the world. *Triton* was the first of the type, launched in 1937. The following year, *Thetis* took to the water. After preliminary trials of the new boat revealed a problem with the hydroplanes, builder Cammell Laird worked on her during the winter and spring.

In June 1939, the submarine was declared ready for her first dive in Liverpool Bay. For this occasion, an unusually large group of guests and observers had swelled the numbers on board from 52 to 103. As was the custom, the builder had provided refreshments for the guests; the weather was excellent and a good time was anticipated by all.

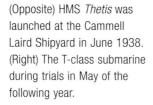

(Opposite) HMS *Thetis* was launched at the Cammell Laird Shipyard in June 1938. (Right) The T-class submarine during trials in May of the following year.

At 1:40 P.M. on June 1, the submarine's captain, Lieutenant Commander Guy Bolus, signaled his intention of diving for three hours. Observers on the escort vessel *Grebecock* watched and were puzzled when, instead of submerging, the submarine floated bow-down for about thirty minutes — looking for all the world as if she were testing the water. What had happened? One possibility was that the submarine was too light: she needed the weight of the water in her torpedo tubes, as well as in her tanks, in order to dive.

Aboard the *Thetis*, Bolus promptly ordered a check of whether the boat was carrying enough water. Because she was light, he had ordered the bowcaps for No. 5 and No. 6 tubes to be opened to flood the two bottom torpedo tubes. Lieutenant Frederick G. Woods, the torpedo officer, went forward to investigate. He checked each tube by opening the test cocks on the rear doors to look for water. Only No. 6 tube had any water in it. Unknown to the torpedo officer, the test cock for No. 5 tube

Period photographs of a typical fore-ends of a Royal Navy submarine, taken during the 1930s. (Above) Crewmen load a torpedo through a bulkhead door into No. 4 torpedo tube. The rear doors of No. 5 and No. 6 tubes are below deck level and very awkward to reach. At sea, one of the bulkhead doorways (right) was kept shut and secure at all times.

was plugged with paint — and so it indicated a dry tube when, in fact, the tube was flooded. A painter had recently given the inside of the tube door a coat of enamel but had neglected to protect the test cock hole and had simply painted over it, covering up the tiny but vital aperture.

Woods then checked to make sure the bowcap for each torpedo tube was shut. There were indicators to show this, but a metal bar partially obscured them and they were hard to see. Instead, Woods checked the levers for the bowcaps. These themselves created problems. The levers for the bowcaps on tubes five and six worked opposite to the other four — that is, when all the levers were lined up, torpedo tubes one through four were closed, while five and six were open. The likelihood is that Woods looked at the levers, saw they all lined up, and believed all was well. The only thing between the interior of the *Thetis* and the sea was the rear door of No. 5 tube.

Woods then ordered a seaman to check each torpedo tube by opening it. The first four were opened and found empty. The fifth seemed a little stiff. When the two men finally turned the handle, water gushed into the compartment, gallons and gallons of it, through the twenty-one-inch torpedo tube now open to the sea.

The *Thetis* suddenly dived. Men stumbled and fell headlong. Loose equipment tumbled, clattering, jangling. Eardrums stung as the air pressure soared. Men clung to whatever happened to be at hand: stanchions, pipes, levers, anything substantial. The vessel rocked, lurching as it dropped through the water. A moment later, the bow hit bottom, 150 feet down. She hung there, immobile, angled at forty degrees, stuck in the silt and sand like a huge arrow that had missed its mark.

The crew tried blowing high-pressure air into her main ballast tank. It didn't help. Water continued to cascade into the torpedo room. If the flooding could be confined to that area, they could still save her. But the men couldn't close the watertight door between the tube space and the torpedo stowage compartment because of the awkward securing arrangement. The angle of the sunken submarine made it impossible; and one of the no less than eighteen separate turnbuckles was jammed. The crew retreated to the next compartment, where they succeeded in closing the watertight hatch.

How a Submarine Dives and Surfaces

A submarine can dive or surface at will because it controls its own buoyancy with ballast tanks. On the surface, a sub's ballast tanks are filled with air.

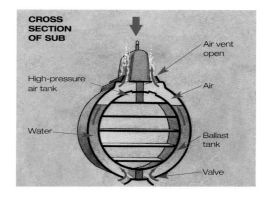

CROSS SECTION OF SUB

High-pressure air tank
Air vent open
Air
Water
Ballast tank
Valve

Going Down: When the submarine dives, water floods the ballast tanks as the air in the tanks is vented out of the sub. Once the vessel is heavier than the surrounding water (negative buoyancy), it sinks.

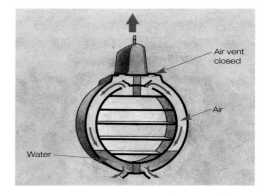

Air vent closed
Air
Water

Going Up: When the sub surfaces, compressed air flows into the ballast tanks as the water is forced out. Once the submarine's overall density is less than the surrounding water (positive buoyancy), the vessel rises.

Confusion and incompetence on the surface added to the submariners' problems. The tug *Grebecock* had anchored over the spot where it was believed the submarine had gone down. But this was some four miles from where the *Thetis* had actually struck the seabed. Compounding the mess, the Royal Air Force had misreported — by an incredible seven miles — the position of a marker buoy.

The *Thetis* was equipped with two indicator buoys operated manually from within the submarine. When released, the buoys would rise to the surface, attached to the submarine by wire. In addition, two underwater guns were provided; they fired "grenades" that set off a flare when they reached the surface to signal a problem. A few minutes before four in the afternoon, Bolus ordered red grenades fired.

The trapped sailors told themselves that as soon as the *Grebecock* spotted the buoys and the red flares, rescue operations would snap into high gear. What the crew couldn't know was that the after buoy had never reached the surface; it had wrapped itself around the submarine's stern. The forward buoy had broken away and was carried off by the strong current.

By now, much of the forward part of the *Thetis* was flooded. But all was not yet lost. The T-class boats were among the first designed with a new escape chamber that allowed crewmembers to escape a sunken submarine using a Davis Submerged Escape Apparatus (DSEA). The chamber had been designed with two main entrances — one opening on each side of the watertight bulkhead that now stood between the flooded portions and the rest of the submarine. Perhaps, one of the crew suggested, the escape chamber might also provide a way of saving the sunken sub. If a man fitted with a Davis escape apparatus could use the chamber to enter the flooded area, he could close the jammed watertight door — and the water in the forward section could then be pumped out. The plan was risky — there was only a thirty-minute supply of oxygen in the Davis gear — but it just might work. Hope stirred like a fresh breeze blowing through the increasingly foul atmosphere on the submarine. The first lieutenant volunteered. After donning the escape gear, he entered the chamber and the water gushed in. It had risen almost to head height when he signaled that he was in distress and had to get out. When he did so, he was sick and dizzy, in agony from the high pressure of the water. Others tried — but they, too, failed.

And then there was the added problem of disposing of the water in the rescue chamber. It soon became clear that the only way to accomplish this was by hand, a line of crewmembers passing bucketsful of water aft. It was a time-consuming, laborious job that taxed the men's strength and gobbled up precious oxygen. Bolus abandoned the plan. The only hope of emptying the flooded

The After Escape Chamber

(Opposite, far right) The escape chamber of a British T-class submarine. Circular doors allowed access from either side. The boxes stacked in front contain DSEA sets. (Opposite) The escape procedure was simple. (Top) Wearing Davis escape gear — the British version of the Momsen Lung — a crewmember enters the escape chamber and closes the watertight door behind him. (Middle) He releases the clip on the upper hatch, then opens a valve to flood the chamber with seawater. (Bottom) Once the chamber is flooded, the crewman pushes open the upper hatch and swims to the surface. After the chamber is emptied of water, another crewmember enters and repeats the procedure.

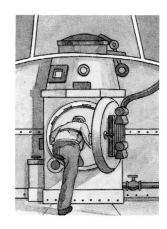

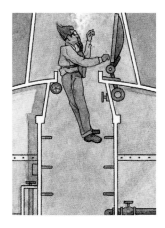

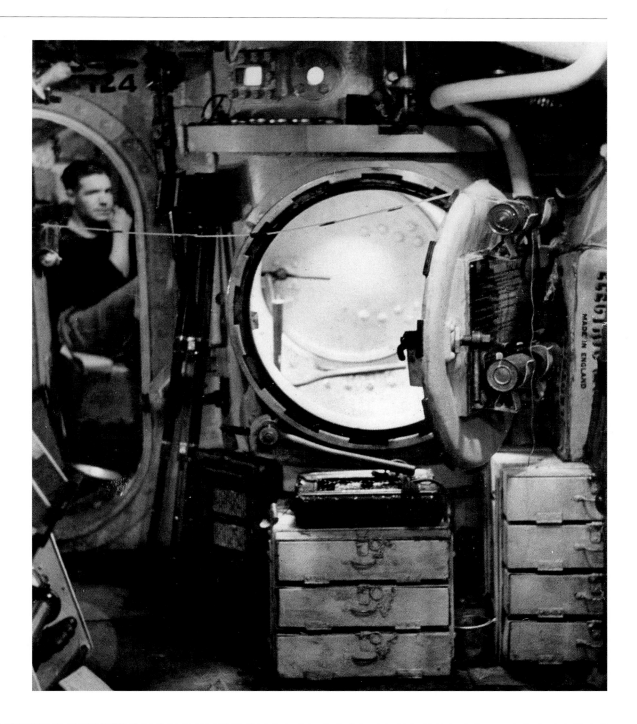

compartment and making the *Thetis* light enough to rise was to get sufficient air from the surface to blow it out.

There was nothing for the occupants of the submarine to do now but wait and try to conserve their remaining strength. By eight in the evening, there was no sign of activity on the surface. The world seemed to have forgotten about them. Moment by moment, the men were slipping into a deadly torpor, finding it harder and harder to concentrate on the problems at hand. The remaining air was becoming staler and fouler. The men settled down to an uneasy night. They would try the escape chamber again the next day.

(Above) Rescue ships converge on the protruding stern of the sunken *Thetis* (roughly in center of photograph) moments after it was spotted in the water.

After the last of the survivors had been plucked from the water, ropes were attached to the stern of the submarine (top left) and a tug attempted to hoist it up (lower left and right) so that divers could enter the stricken vessel.

In the morning, the crew of the destroyer *Brazen* spotted the submarine's stern protruding from the water and hurried to her side. To their amazement, two men emerged from the depths — Captain H.P. Oram, commander of the Fifth Submarine Flotilla and one of the guests on board, and Lieutenant Woods, the torpedo officer. Both were wearing Davis escape gear. An hour or so later, two more men appeared: Leading Stoker Walter Arnold and Frank Shaw, a Cammell Laird fitter. The survivors reported on conditions aboard the *Thetis*. It was getting worse by the hour. The men were weak and disoriented, and some had already slipped into unconsciousness. They could not last much longer.

Meanwhile, down below, something else had gone terribly wrong. The sailor in charge of the escape chamber, no doubt dazed and barely conscious, failed to release the gearing on the upper hatch; now it could no longer be opened from within. Then he forgot to turn off the flooding valve when he returned to the motor room. It was the end. The sea rushed in, pushing up the already critical carbon dioxide level. The ninety-nine men still alive on the *Thetis* slipped into unconsciousness. Soon they all died, quietly, painlessly.

Above, the rescue efforts continued — as did the run of bad luck that had plagued the *Thetis* since its sinking. Just as divers were attempting to gain entry to the submarine, the weather suddenly worsened and the wires connecting the *Thetis* to a rescue tug snapped. With a sickening splash, the submarine slipped from sight.

(Top) After the *Thetis* was raised and salvaged, it was grounded ashore at Moelfre Bay on September 3, 1939 — the day that Britain declared war on Germany. (Above, left and right) The *Thetis* during salvage.

Both the *Thetis* and the *Squalus* were raised and extensively rebuilt, then pressed into wartime service. The *Thetis* became HMS *Thunderbolt* and served well in the Mediterranean until she was sunk with all hands by an Italian escort ship off the coast of Sicily on March 14, 1943. The *Squalus* was relaunched as the USS *Sailfish* and enjoyed a successful career in the Pacific. In December 1943, she sank a Japanese carrier and later stopped to pick up survivors. Incredibly, among them were some men from the USS *Sculpin*, taken prisoner by the Japanese only a month before.

The HMS *Thunderbolt* (below, left). (Bottom left) Commissioning ceremonies for the USS *Sailfish* (right).

Chapter Six: **The U-boat War**

They lie today, some 780 of them — most with the remains of their crews still aboard — scattered along the North Atlantic seabed between the West Indies and Norway. Some sit upright, others are askew, their flat decks disappearing into the muddy seabed. They are the greatest single fleet of lost submarines in history. Under the imaginative but unpretentious Admiral Karl Dönitz, they and their sister U-boats came very close to buying Germany the victory that had eluded her in the First World War. Now they are slowly rusting away, returning to the base elements from which men fashioned them more than sixty years ago.

Maritime artist John Hamilton captures the *U-309* on patrol in the North Atlantic.

Although the Allied admirals knew how few submarines the Germans possessed at the outbreak of war in September 1939, they had no idea how formidable the small U-boat force was. Had they known, they would have been flabbergasted. Both Britain and France had amassed substantial fleets: the British could boast about fifty subs, the French about seventy. By contrast, Germany had only thirty-nine fully operational U-boats — although Hitler kept assuring his commander that he would soon have many more. But what Dönitz lacked in numbers he more than made up for in quality, combined with superb training and dedicated personnel. Dönitz personally selected every man and made him undergo a training regimen that became notorious. Only the best stayed the course. It may have been an ordeal to qualify for Dönitz's command, but no man wanted to transfer out. To become a member of the *U-bootwaffe* was to join an elite force, admired throughout the nation. U-boat men were the best paid in the German services. They rated themselves as the most efficient submariners in the world. Under Dönitz's careful control, these crews and their boats were poised to function as a unified powerful weapon. And they would revolutionize the way the submarine was used in combat.

Karl Dönitz (above) was given responsibility in 1935 for building up Germany's new U-boat fleet. He masterminded all the tactics the U-boats used throughout the war — including the "wolf pack" attacks on convoys.

Declaration of War

Less than twelve hours after Britain declared war on Germany on September 3, 1939, the commander of *U-30* mistook the liner SS *Athenia* for a troopship and sank her without warning. One hundred and twelve passengers perished, including a number of Americans. The world was outraged — especially since U-boats had sworn to observe the internationally accepted Prize Rules governing warfare at sea. Anxious to mollify the United States, the German Propaganda Ministry immediately declared that Winston Churchill was behind the sinking — deliberately planned by Britain to incriminate Germany. (Right) Survivors from the *Athenia*.

With the outbreak of war, U-boat construction in Germany escalated dramatically. Nineteen shipyards in eleven cities, including Hamburg, Kiel and Wilhelmshaven, built the 1,174 submarines that were eventually launched. By 1942, U-boats were also docked in fortified pens in France (left). U-boat crews raise the new war flag of the Third Reich (above) and prepare for inspection (top and bottom).

"The knowledge acquired during this single year of training, in which the crews were tested to the limits of human endeavor, was the foundation…upon which the future structure of the U-boat Arm was built."

— A U-boat commander comments on Karl Dönitz's training program

Honing a **Weapon of War**

Karl Dönitz revolutionized the U-boat training program to reflect the way in which he viewed the submarines themselves — as the most effective weapon of war available to Germany. From his U-boat elite, he demanded both complete enthusiasm and complete faith. During hundreds of exhaustive training attacks, his crews learned to handle their craft in enemy waters, surfaced and submerged, inshore and offshore. They perfected stalking techniques for use in daytime and at night. And they became superbly skilled at anticipating enemy movements during tactical attacks, particularly by convoys or by enemy aircraft.

(Right) Naval artist Randall Wilson depicted the British carrier HMS *Courageous* on fire after torpedo hits from the *U-29*. Two Swordfish aircraft fly past the stricken vessel.

Dönitz's submariners didn't take long to start chalking up notable victories. The first came on September 17. The 22,500-ton aircraft carrier HMS *Courageous* was on antisubmarine patrol off the Irish coast in the western approaches to the English Channel. Eight Swordfish aircraft had set out in response to a report that the steamer *Kafiristan* had been attacked by a U-boat. The search had revealed nothing and, with their fuel getting low, the aircraft headed back to rejoin the carrier.

The last of the patrolling Swordfish smacked down on the carrier's deck and its three-man crew clambered out — just as *U-29* launched three torpedoes. Two scored hits. Smoke and spray erupted from the *Courageous* as chunks of steel and fragments of equipment toppled into the sea. In minutes, the carrier began to capsize and scores of sailors leapt into the oil-fouled water. More than five hundred of the ship's twelve hundred officers and men went down with the *Courageous*.

It was an impressive first blow for the U-boat force, but the next outdid it. Dönitz had for some time been contemplating an attack on Scapa Flow in the Orkney Islands to the north of Scotland. The rocky and forbidding place was the base of the British Home Fleet. It was barricaded against ships by an impenetrable wall of rocks, rusting hulks, cables and other obstacles — most of them positioned during the previous war, when the Admiralty had had nightmares about the possibility of enemy intruders. Dönitz wondered just how impenetrable the defenses really were. Perhaps the slim form of a U-boat might be able to wend its way through the various obstacles. He examined aerial photographs and found one channel, named Kirk Sound, that had a gap of about fifty feet — enough for a U-boat to slide through.

Even as his plans were still taking shape, Dönitz had already decided who should command such an audacious expedition. Günther Prien, a thirty-one-year-old former merchant officer, had already shown himself to be an excellent submariner who knew his boat and his crew inside out. In the war's first days, he had sunk the British freighter *Bosnia* and two other merchantmen. On October 1, Dönitz told Prien about the proposed foray. As Dönitz had anticipated, the young submariner was enthusiastic.

Seven days later, Prien's *U-47* — a Type VIIB U-boat — slipped quietly from its berth at Wilhelmshaven, purring along the canal to the sea. Prien had already told his crew about their mission. Their reaction delighted him. If enthusiasm and courage counted for anything, the job was as good as done. The name Scapa Flow had a particular significance for the German crew. It was there that the German High Seas Fleet had been assembled at the end of the First World War — and it was there that the crews scuttled the Kaiser's dreadnoughts, rather than surrendering the German fleet to the victorious Allies.

During the daylight hours, the *U-47* hid on the ocean floor like some enormous crustacean waiting for its prey. At night the monster stirred, pumping out ballast, then easing out of the silt and cautiously surfacing after a meticulous scanning of the area by hydrophone.

At last Prien entered Kirk Sound, the start of the nerve-wracking journey into the heart of the anchorage. The *U-47*'s steel hull scraped the sides and bottom of the narrow passage. Prien stared out into the waters of the sound. Incredibly, he could see no battleships. Was he in the wrong place?

His doubts grew as he made his way into the fifteen-mile-long strip of water. He glanced up at the moon. It was uncommonly bright; in fact, the whole area was illuminated by the aurora borealis, giving the scene an oddly theatrical look. Prien thought briefly of postponing the mission and waiting for better conditions. But he decided to push on. Although he grounded the *U-47* briefly and at one point found himself heading into the wrong stretch of water, he eventually succeeded in reaching Scapa Flow.

Günther Prien (below) used a powerful Type VIIB U-boat — shown (opposite, bottom) in profile and overhead — for his bold foray into Scapa Flow. (Opposite, top) An aerial view of Scapa Flow today, with the Churchill Barriers stretching across the water to the left and right.

SIDE VIEW

TOP VIEW

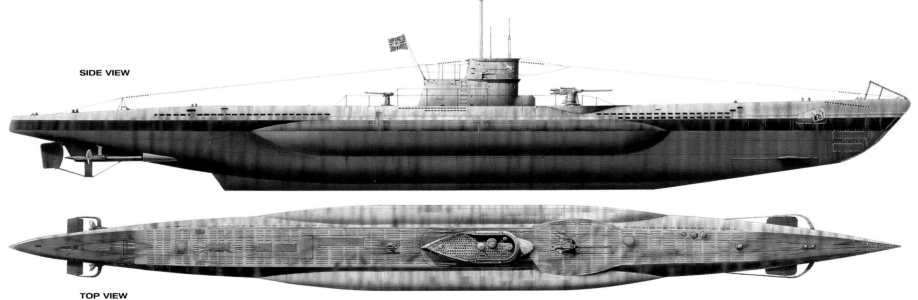

Again, everything seemed eerily quiet. There should have been dozens of ships all over the place. Suddenly, out of the misty shadows, two ships took shape. Large ships. Important ships, by the look of them. With the assistance of his first officer, Engelbert Endrass, Prien identified them as the *Royal Oak* and the *Repulse*, a battleship and a battle cruiser respectively. (In fact, Prien correctly identified only one ship, the *Royal Oak*, an aging veteran of the Battle of Jutland in 1916. The second ship was not the *Repulse*, but a seaplane transport, the *Pegasus*.) At 12:55 A.M., Prien fired four torpedoes, two at each ship. Only one found its mark, hitting the *Royal Oak* near the bow and blowing a fifty-foot-wide hole along the waterline. The captain, wakened from his sleep, grumpily ordered an inspection, after which he concluded that spontaneous combustion had caused a minor explosion in the paint locker. No one had been hurt; the ship's watertight doors had sealed off the damaged section. Everyone went back to bed.

"Here is the news bulletin. As it was reported late this morning, the Secretary of the Admiralty regrets to announce that HMS *Royal Oak* has been sunk, it is believed, by U-boat action." — The BBC Home Service, October 14, 1939

Aboard the U-boat, Günther Prien was puzzled by the lack of reaction. He had expected the whole base to be on full alert by now, with floodlights sweeping the water and flares punctuating the night sky. Instead, a peaceful, almost sleepy, scene confronted him. Prien fired his stern torpedo but missed; it ended up on shore. Then, with the possibility of abysmal failure staring him in the face, he launched his last three torpedoes.

All three hit the *Royal Oak*, blowing the ship's starboard flank to pieces. A magazine exploded, setting off a furious blaze. One torpedo struck the engine room. The old battleship, trembling as if in pain, slowly rolled over to starboard. A mighty explosion heaved her almost into the air. Her enormous hulk created a minor tidal wave when it crashed back into the water. Suddenly, convulsively, she turned turtle, taking with her more than eight hundred of her twelve-hundred-man crew.

Prien made for the sea, convinced that British destroyers were in pursuit. Two and a half hours after entering Scapa Flow, he was back in open water. But no pursuers panted behind him. In fact, there was no sign that anyone was the least upset by his exploit. He could scarcely believe his luck!

When *U-47* arrived back at Wilhelmshaven, an elated Dönitz was waiting on the quay with Admiral Erich Raeder, the head of the Kriegsmarine. Iron Crosses were awarded to every member of

(Above) Admiral Dönitz presents Iron Crosses to the crew of the *U-47*. (Opposite) A diver swims through the wrecks that were deliberately sunk in Scapa Flow to deter enemy intruders. (Inset, top) The barnacle-covered antiaircraft guns of HMS *Royal Oak* and its propeller shaft (bottom), draped with a British battle flag.

the crew, including the Iron Cross First Class for Prien. Hitler sent his personal aircraft to fly everyone to Berlin, where the entire city turned out to greet the heroes. He also promoted Dönitz to the rank of admiral, in recognition of the brilliant and audacious Scapa Flow incursion. In London, a grim-faced Winston Churchill stood up in Parliament and admitted that Prien's exploit was remarkable. Then he went to Scapa Flow and ordered the camouflaging of the oil tanks and the building of dummy oil facilities for the Luftwaffe to waste its bombs on. He also ordered the firing of Sir William French, the flag officer in command of Shetland and Orkney. (Interestingly, the reason Prien found so few warships in Scapa Flow was that most of them had gone in pursuit of the German cruisers *Gneisenau* and *Köln*. Only the *Royal Oak* had returned to Scapa Flow after the unsuccessful chase; the others had put in at Loch Ewe.)

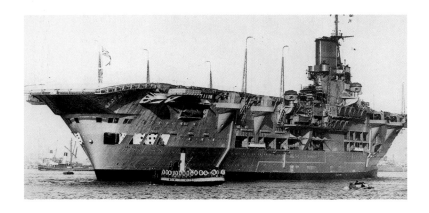

(Above) The British aircraft carrier HMS *Ark Royal*.

Two important warships sunk in as many weeks was a major accomplishment for the U-boat fleet. But serious technical problems had prevented a third triumph. Three days before the *Courageous* was sunk, *U-39*, a Type IX U-boat under the command of Gerhard Glattes, wound up with the aircraft carrier *Ark Royal* in its sights. Glattes had fired a fan of three torpedoes — but all of them inexplicably failed. The *Ark Royal* retaliated with depth charges that forced the unlucky U-boat to the surface. Its officers and crew were taken prisoner — the first U-boat loss of the war.

Torpedo problems continued to plague the U-boats. In the spring of 1940, during the Norwegian campaign, Günther Prien was patrolling in the vicinity of Bygden Fjord when he came across a very tempting target — half a dozen transports escorted by two cruisers. Prien planned his attack meticulously. He would make his approach in the *U-47* submerged, then surface and fire four bow torpedoes, reload the forward tubes and escape after firing more torpedoes. It would be the greatest, most devastating U-boat attack in history. Unfortunately, not a single torpedo worked. One hit a cliff; the others simply vanished. In his fury and frustration, Prien ran onto a sandbar, and it took hours to get the *U-47* free. To make matters worse, the starboard diesel failed under the strain. Prien aborted the patrol and went back to base to complain vociferously to Dönitz.

After months of investigation, it became apparent that the fault lay with the torpedo detonators.

(Above and right) Crewmen in the torpedo room of a German submarine. Maintaining the weapons in a constant state of readiness was dirty work and included moving the torpedoes every day, reloading them after firing and keeping all parts serviced and batteries charged.

There were two torpedo types: magnetic, and contact. The former, used against heavily armored targets, had detonators designed to be activated by the magnetic field of their target's hull. This generated a current in a coil that exploded the warhead. But the weapons proved notoriously unreliable in service; most magnetic torpedoes simply passed under their targets without exploding. Others exploded prematurely, affected perhaps by the proximity of the North Pole and by iron ore lodes beneath the seabed. The simpler contact detonator, essentially a percussion cap, was generally used for so-called "soft-skinned" targets such as merchant ships. The trouble was, the twin-bladed trigger on the nose would work only if it struck the target at precisely ninety degrees. The Germans solved that problem by capturing a British torpedo and copying its detonator mechanism.

But the investigation into torpedo malfunctions revealed additional problems. Wartime service meant that torpedoes — immensely complicated weapons packed with a great deal of delicate equipment — were constantly on the move and often subjected to extreme changes in temperature and pressure. Such conditions played havoc with the torpedo's systems. The chamber for the hydrostatic valve that controlled the torpedo's horizontal steering fins, for instance, was not airtight. Changes in air pressure brought about by repeated dives and other maneuvers also affected the weapon's accuracy. A full-scale inquiry led to six months' imprisonment for the man in charge of torpedo development, Rear Admiral Oskar Wehr. Thereafter, the quality of the Kriegsmarine's torpedoes began to improve.

Despite the problems with their torpedoes, Dönitz's U-boats were still cutting a swath through Britain's shipping. The Royal Navy had reintroduced the convoy system for merchant ships at the outbreak of the war, and for the first few months, shipping losses had averaged eighty thousand tons a month — serious, but by no means catastrophic. But from June to December 1940, Dönitz's U-boats sank an average of 240,000 tons a month. This shocking tally was directly attributable to the availability of excellent French bases in Lorient and, later, in St. Nazaire, Brest, La Pallice and La Rochelle — all of which fell into German hands with the French surrender.

The Germans discovered to their considerable delight that Lorient provided repair facilities superior to those in Germany — but the greatest benefit was geographical. Prior to July 1940, U-boats had to travel 450 miles through the North Sea and around the north of Great Britain to reach the Atlantic. Now, thanks to the bases in France, they were able to save about a week on the trip. Dönitz, in his typically methodical way, calculated that the use of the French facilities and their proximity to the battle areas represented a twenty-two percent increase in his force without the addition of a single U-boat. Dönitz also benefited greatly from the able work of B-Dienst, the German Navy's decoding department, which provided him with consistently accurate information on Allied convoy movements.

Perhaps the most astonishing thing about the U-boat campaign was that during the period June to December 1940 — which veteran U-boat men remember fondly as *die Glückliche Zeit* (the Happy Time) — there were rarely more than a dozen U-boats in the Atlantic on any given day. No wonder Dönitz believed that if only he were given the force he wanted, he could win the war for Germany.

(Left) A new British cargo ship under construction. As the U-boat war escalated, British shipyards frantically tried to keep pace with the demand for new merchant vessels. Ships that normally took over a year to build were now assembled — in a much simplified form — in six to eight months.

(Above, left) A U-boat crew heads back to home port. (Right) On the lookout for merchant ships.

In the fall of 1940, he put into effect some of his "wolf pack" theories (known as *Rudeltaktik* to the Germans). Under Dönitz's direction, groups of U-boats took up positions across convoy routes. The British escorts were using the ASDIC underwater detection system, which could detect a nearby submarine and tell the listener how far away it was. Unfortunately, the system worked only if a sub was underwater — a shortcoming that Dönitz turned to his advantage. He had his U-boats tail their intended victims by day and then surface to attack at night.

Typically, several U-boats attacked simultaneously, swamping the escort force. Many convoys were savagely mauled by the U-boats — some of which penetrated to the heart of the convoy, then sailed along the rows of merchantmen, sinking them one after another. One U-boat ace, Joachim Schepke, in command of *U-100*, slipped into the middle of a convoy and sank seven ships, totaling over fifty thousand tons. In October 1940, one convoy suffered the catastrophic loss of thirty-two of its thirty-five ships — nearly two hundred thousand tons of shipping in all.

Dönitz ran this huge operation almost single-handedly, directing his forces by radio. By the end of 1940, he was instructing his skippers to transmit sightings of convoys to headquarters by

> "It is essential, in an attack on any given objective, to be able to deliver the attack in as great strength as possible.... A massed target, then, should be attacked by massed U-boats."
>
> — Admiral Karl Dönitz, on his wolf pack tactics

radio so that reinforcements could be directed if required, and Dönitz could follow the action minute by minute. Eventually, however, the U-boat commander's increasing use of radio communication exacted a price. The British were able to learn a great deal about the movements of U-boats from the constant interchange within Dönitz's command.

Another strike against Germany's submarine force came in August 1941 (although the Germans did not know it at the time). Britain's decryption experts at Bletchley Park near London chalked up a major victory by breaking the code used by the German Navy. The British, careful not to give their advantage away, kept their convoys out of trouble simply by re-routing them. The Germans, in turn, were puzzled by the lack of action but not particularly suspicious. In the long-established thrust and parry of naval war, one side could gain a brief advantage, only to relinquish it later in favor of the other side. For their part, German code-breakers succeeded in penetrating the Royal Navy's main operational codes and were well on their way to breaking the naval code used jointly by Britain, Canada and the still neutral United States for convoy operations.

(Right) John Hamilton's evocative painting documents the destruction wrought by one of Dönitz's wolf packs after it had penetrated a convoy of merchant ships.

Escape from the **Perseus**

John Capes' escape from HMS *Perseus* (left) is one of the more remarkable stories of luck and courage aboard submarines during World War II. Capes (inset), a navy stoker, was hitching a ride on the *Perseus* the night of December 6, 1941, when the British submarine struck a mine while on patrol in the Ionian Sea. The damage was immediate — and devastating. Water flooded the vessel, and within minutes the sub had nosedived to the bottom of the sea, killing most of the crew. Capes, although hurt, miraculously survived the sinking — as did, briefly, three other badly injured stokers. With amazing strength and coolheadedness, he managed to get the escape hatch open, but by then the remaining survivors

had either died or lapsed into unconsciousness. Only Capes made it out of the flooded submarine and into the open sea. Using his Davis escape gear as a lifebelt of sorts, he swam for several hours in the bitterly cold waters before collapsing on a beach on the Greek island of Cephalonia. Villagers found him the next morning and sheltered him for eighteen months before smuggling him to safety in Turkey. In 1998, Greek diver Kostas Thoctarides (who took the photo opposite) found the wreck of the *Perseus*, with the escape hatch open — just as Capes left it. Everything in the stern compartment was as the lucky stoker had described it, including the bottle of rum that Capes had been enjoying just minutes before the mine exploded. It probably helped save his life. John Capes died in 1985 at the age of 75.

In the second half of 1941, two enormously important developments altered the course of the war: the Germans invaded Soviet Russia, and the Japanese attacked the United States Fleet at Pearl Harbor. The possibility of war with the United States had occupied Dönitz's mind for some time. He had developed a plan for a U-boat attack on the North American continent — *Paukenschlag* (Operation Drumbeat). Unfortunately for Dönitz, Hitler chose that moment to have one of his periodic panics about Norway, which Germany had occupied since the spring of 1940. Convinced that the Allies intended to invade, he demanded that Dönitz shift more U-boats to Norway to guard the coast — reducing the number available for *Paukenschlag* to a mere half-dozen Type IX long-distance boats, half the number Dönitz had originally planned. Eventually, only five boats set sail for America.

On January 2, 1942, the British Admiralty first warned Washington of the strong possibility of a U-boat offensive on the American east coast. The intelligence came from Enigma decrypts. But it fell on deaf ears. When the first of the U-boats arrived off the North American coast, there was nothing to indicate that the United States was at war. The submariners stared in amazement at the illuminated shoreline and at the ships moving along the coast, apparently unconcerned about the possibility of attack.

Dönitz realized that five submarines were not going to send the Americans down to defeat; however, properly employed, they could certainly create a lot of trouble. He scattered his force over a large area of water, from the St. Lawrence estuary in the north to North Carolina's Cape Hatteras in the south.

The first casualty of the campaign was the 9,000-ton British merchantman *Cyclops*, sunk by *U-123* south of Cape Cod, Massachusetts, on January 12. It was the beginning of an extraordinary slaughter, much of it carried out within sight of the shore — and, in fact, often watched by vacationers sipping cocktails on beaches in Florida, Georgia, the Carolinas and the Caribbean. The bright backdrop provided by America's cities and

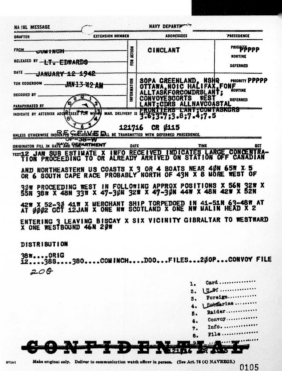

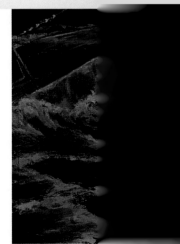

(Above) The intelligence summary of U-boat positions and courses sent by the British Admiralty to the US Navy Department in Washington on January 12, 1942. (Right) A U-boat attack in American waters during the first days of Operation Drumbeat, by artist Anthony Saunders.

beach resorts made the job that much easier for the U-boats by silhouetting their victims. Surprisingly, none of the naval and military commanders called for any form of blackout. Admiral Adolphus Andrews, responsible for coastal defense in the northeast, had comforting words for all: "The lights of beach resorts frequently furnish a background against which vessels running close to the coast may be silhouetted by others further seaward. This is objectionable, but inasmuch as submarines are reluctant to operate in waters less than about ten fathoms in depth, this is not at present regarded as creating a problem requiring drastic measures."

At the time, no convoy system operated on the American east coast. Admiral Ernest King, the senior naval commander, was of the opinion that an inadequate naval escort was worse than no escort at all. King was faced with the same shortage of escort vessels that plagued the Royal Navy; the United States Navy found itself in a war on two major fronts and had not adequately prepared for either.

By January 13, the last of the five U-boats had reached their assigned positions: *U-123* near the eastern tip of Long Island, *U-125* off New Jersey, and *U-66* off Cape Hatteras, North Carolina. *U-123* sank the 9,600-ton Panamanian tanker *Norness* — then headed toward New York for a look at the city's bright lights! In the early hours of the following morning, she sank the British tanker *Coimbra*, which was on its way to Halifax, Nova Scotia. The 6,768-ton vessel

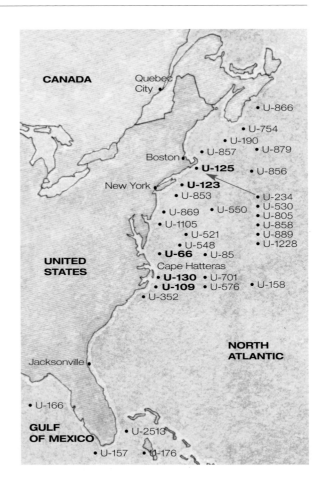

(Above) A map detailing the extent of the U-boat offensive on the American east coast — including the initial surprise attack, Operation Drumbeat, in mid-January 1942 (the five participating subs are shown in bold on the map).

blew up in a ghastly fireball clearly visible from the shore. Thirty-six of the forty-two men on board perished. Aircraft, blimps and a variety of small craft set off in pursuit of the daring submarine. Their enthusiasm was admirable but the crews lacked experience in sub-hunting. Reinhard Hardegen, commander of the *U-123*, dismissed the US Navy as "a paper fleet.... Its commanders were either incompetent or negligent or both."

The five U-boats quickly sank about a quarter of a million tons of shipping in American and Canadian waters — without losing one of their number. Dönitz noted in his war diary that the Americans were "wholly lacking in experience. Single destroyers, for example, sailed up and down the traffic lanes with such regularity that the U-boats were quickly able to work out the timetable being followed. They knew exactly when the destroyers would return, and the knowledge only added to their sense of security during the intervening period. A few attacks with depth charges were delivered by American patrol vessels, but the attackers did not display the requisite perseverance, and the attacks were abandoned too quickly — although quite often, thanks to the shallow water, they stood a good chance of succeeding. The aircraft crews employed on antisubmarine work were also untrained." In a matter of months, however, Dönitz's opinion of the Americans' abilities would change.

In mid-May 1942, as the waves of U-boat attacks continued, the US Navy introduced a convoy system on the eastern seaboard — and, belatedly, blackout measures. More escort vessels were also now available, thanks to a construction program President Roosevelt had set in motion a year earlier. Soon, three U-boats were sunk along the American east coast and two more were damaged. On July 16, Dönitz withdrew the last of his boats from American waters.

(Above) A New York housewife receives instructions on hanging blackout curtains. Even Broadway was affected by the blackout restrictions along the east coast, as depicted in *Times Square Dim-Out* (right) by artist James W. Kerr. (Below) Marines with their guard dogs patrol a Florida beach.

US Coast Guard Captures **German Sub**

Shortly after the first wave of German U-boats arrived off the American east coast during Operation Drumbeat, a number of Coast Guard cutters joined the flotilla of small naval craft and private boats patrolling the coastal waters. These submarine chasers also routinely aided in the rescue of hundreds of men from torpedoed American vessels, particularly in the busy shipping lanes off North Carolina. On May 9, 1942, a Coast Guard cutter once again came to the rescue of men at sea — but this time, it was the crew of a scuttled German sub. The 165-foot cutter *Icarus* had spotted the *U-352*, which had arrived in American waters only a week earlier, and proceeded to depth-charge the unlucky U-boat. After the survivors were picked out of the water, the *Icarus* delivered them to the Charleston Navy Yard — the first POWs taken by the United States after the declaration of war with Germany. Lieutenant Maurice D. Jester, commander of the *Icarus*, was awarded the Navy Cross for his actions in sinking the larger, faster and more heavily armed sub.

(Opposite) The ghostly wreck of the *U-352*. (Inset) Hellmut Rathke, commander of the *U-352*, and his men come ashore from the *Icarus* for processing before being transferred to a military prison. (This page) Underwater photographer Brian Skerry took these images during a dive to the *U-352* off the North Carolina coast. (Above) Divers approach the rusted conning tower of the German submarine. A human skull (below, left) and the aft end of a torpedo (below, right) encapsulate the final, sad chapter of the *U-352*'s wartime voyage to the United States.

In the intervening months, there had been a striking increase in Dönitz's U-boat strength. By January 1943, he had four hundred U-boats under his command. At one time, such a force would have been sufficient to win the war. But not now.

A remarkable variety of antisubmarine gadgetry now flowed from factories in Britain and the United States. Perhaps the most important was the development of the cavity magnetron by British scientists. It paved the way for the introduction of the "ten centimeter" radar — the ASV Mark III — which could detect surfaced submarines at twelve miles. Other invaluable equipment included MAD (Magnetic Anomaly Detector) — an offshoot of the magnetometer, widely used in the mining industry to locate underground mineral deposits. The antisubmarine version relied on the fact that the passage of a submarine through water caused changes in the earth's magnetic field. The equipment was usually carried in aircraft, often PBYs, the US Navy's workhorse flying boats — also known as Catalinas in the British service, with the MAD-carrying versions known inevitably as MADCats.

One of MAD's great advantages was that, unlike sonar, its signal did not create a distinct "ping" when it bounced off the hull — so submarines had no clue that they had been detected. Unfortunately, MAD-equipped aircraft had to be directly over a submarine in order to fix its position accurately. By then, it was too late to drop a conventional depth charge that would hit the water anywhere near the sub — so the aircraft were armed with "retro bombs." When launched, a small solid-fuel rocket propelled the retro bomb backward. Then on burnout, the bomb fell vertically onto the target.

The aircrews also had no way of determining whether the MAD equipment was actually detecting a U-boat or the ancient hulk of a tug on the seabed — since both generated the same reading.

This prompted the development of another successful antisubmarine device: the sonobuoy, a small radio transmitter with a hydrophone suspended on a length of line. Whatever sounds the hydrophone picked up were passed to the transmitter on the surface, then to the patrolling aircraft. This was especially effective with aircraft carrying the air-launched homing torpedo — popularly known as "Wandering Annie" or "Fido" — which was fitted with an acoustic device that zeroed in on the "popping" caused by the action of a submarine's propellers.

Surface ships also received an arsenal of new weapons — including the Hedgehog (an "ahead-throwing" weapon that consisted of twenty-four depth charges mounted on six rows of spigots) and the Squid (a three-barrel mortar that fired projectiles, each packed with two hundred pounds of Minol-II, a powerful mixture of Amatol and aluminum).

(Below) U-boats take shape at one of Germany's many shipyards. By the beginning of 1943, an all-out construction effort was providing Admiral Dönitz with twenty new submarines each month.

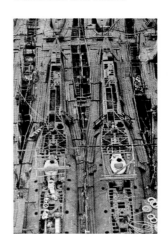

(Top, left) Crewmen aboard a warship load depth-charge projectiles onto a Hedgehog antisubmarine weapon. (Above) Operators aboard the Australian ship HMAS *Rockhampton* use ASDIC (a sonic detection device) to locate an enemy submarine. (Right) A convoy cruiser drops depth charges.

The impact of the new antisubmarine devices was reflected in the ever-growing casualty lists. By 1943, the war under the sea had become grimmer and tougher — although the U-boat crews were still being assured by the propaganda-mongers that they were winning, and that the Allies were just months from collapse. The new generation of U-boats would decimate Allied shipping, they were told. But the revolutionary boats — faster and infinitely more effective — took a long time to develop. In the meantime, the "old reliables," the Type VII and IX U-boats — the backbone of the force since the outbreak of war — got a new lease on life with the introduction of a device its Dutch inventor called the *snuiver,* or "sniffer." Soon it became known as the *Schnorchel* (or "snorkel" in English).

Before long, Dönitz's boats were sporting pairs of pipes — one to suck in air, the other to expel exhaust gases from the diesel engines. This was a major advance in submarine development, and no one could understand why it hadn't been put to use before. For the first time in its history, the submarine was able to operate on diesels under water — and recharge its batteries at the same time. The snorkel device could also be used to bring fresh air into a submerged U-boat, although the procedure was tricky and dangerous (at least two U-boats were lost when they flooded while attempting it).

But the device also presented problems. Operating on diesels was a noisy business — a worrisome shortcoming for U-boat crews who lived in fear of being "overheard" by the enemy. And the boats needed to run close to the surface whenever they employed the snorkel device, which led to control problems. As well, there were frequent breakdowns in the snorkel equipment.

All of these problems were resolved in the new U-boats — Types XXI and XXIII. But by now, the war was drawing to a close. The first Type XXIII went into action in February 1945. *U-2322*, under the command of Fridtjof Heckel, sank a small British merchant ship off eastern Scotland. When escorts gave chase, the U-boat evaded them with ease — thanks to her streamlined design and an underwater speed in excess of twelve knots. In April, a Type XXI U-boat, *U-2511*, put to sea, commanded by Adalbert Schnee. The last word in underwater weaponry, *U-2511* boasted spacious living quarters for the crew and such luxuries as a deep-freeze for the storage of food. Her six torpedo tubes could be reloaded in a few minutes at the press of a button — and with an underwater speed of sixteen knots, the *U-2511* had little to fear from the "killer" groups organized by the Allied navies to hunt U-boats.

If the new U-boats had been introduced earlier, they might have affected the outcome of the war at sea. But the wonder boats were too little, too late. That war was virtually over. So, indeed, was the wider war. German armies were in full retreat on all fronts. On April 30, in Berlin, Hitler formally expelled Hermann Göring from the Nazi party and appointed *Grossadmiral* Dönitz president of the Reich and supreme commander of the armed forces. The Führer committed suicide shortly afterward. The erstwhile U-boat chief claimed to have been taken completely by surprise by the appointment. He declared that he had last spoken to Hitler in July 1944; at that time, the German dictator had given him no clues as to his plans for succession. In any event, it was a dubious honor. The nation was in

By mid-1943, the hard-hitting Allied counteroffensive in the North Atlantic was taking its toll on the U-boat force. (Opposite) *U-185*, shortly after a deadly hit by a Fido acoustic torpedo. (Above) A crewman on a US Coast Guard escort keeps score of U-boat sinkings. (Below) The *U-2511*.

(Above) The surrender of
U-boats at Loch Eriboll off
the Scottish coast, by war
artist Lieutenant Leonard
Frank Brooks.

chaos. Its major cities were little more than rubble. The machinery of state was in shambles.

On May 7, 1945, the date of Germany's surrender, Dönitz ordered his U-boats to surface and set course for the ports specified by the Allies. Most did. Two crews defied the order and scuttled their boats. *U-977* slipped out of a Norwegian fjord and, making use of her snorkel, sailed with her crew halfway around the world. In August, the men attempted to land in Argentina to start a new life — a modern-day *Bounty* escapade. To the sailors' disappointment, the reception was far from cordial. Instead of establishing new homes, they found themselves in Argentinian prisons.

Karl Dönitz, arrested by the victorious Allies, declared that he had nothing to apologize for; he had fought an honorable war. At the Nuremberg trials, the prosecution claimed that he should receive the death penalty for his *Laconia* order forbidding U-boats from rescuing survivors of ships they had sunk. When the American admiral, Chester Nimitz, admitted that the United States Navy had pursued

(Top left) US naval and air vessels escort the *U-858* after its surrender off Cape May, New Jersey. (Above) *U-858*'s commander. (Right) A stack of rusting U-boat torpedoes at the Kiel Shipyard.

a similar policy in the Pacific, the sentence was reduced to ten years' imprisonment. Dönitz served his term in Spandau Prison, Berlin. He died in 1980, apparently still convinced that the naval code had never been broken.

Dönitz's men gave him unquestioning loyalty and maintained an incredible level of morale to the end. Their battle was the biggest, bitterest submarine campaign in history. Some forty thousand German sailors went to war in U-boats. Three out of every four died in action. The courage of the U-boat men never wavered, even when hopes of victory had faded completely. The Germans built 1,174 U-boats between 1939 and 1945. Seven hundred and eighty four were sunk in action. Two hundred more were scuttled by their crews. The Allies took the rest, towed them out to sea, and disposed of them off the west coast of Ireland.

They lie there still.

War in the Pacific

Half a world away, as Germany's U-boats were trying to bring Britain to its knees, the submarines of the United States Navy (aided later by British and Dutch boats) were waging a similar war against the Japanese. America's submarines were the first naval units to take the war to Japan. On December 15, 1941, a little more than a week after Pearl Harbor, the USS *Swordfish* sank its first Japanese merchant ship. Unfortunately, bad torpedoes hobbled the early performance of the American subs in the Pacific — just as they had handicapped the U-boats in the opening months of the Atlantic war. The magnetic Mark XV either ran too deep or circled around, detonated too soon or not at all, did almost anything but explode under its target. After the magnetic warheads were replaced with contact heads in 1943, the torpedo success rate rose dramatically — as did the number of American hits on merchant vessels carrying vital supplies to Japan (above). By the end of the war, America's big fleet submarines (over three hundred feet long, with ten torpedo tubes) dominated the waters off Japan. All told, they accounted for more than five million tons of merchant shipping — almost eighty percent of what Japan had at the beginning of the war. About 214 warships also fell to their guns and torpedoes. Submarines served in other roles, too, notably rescuing downed US airmen — some 504 by war's end. The submarine force (left) in the Pacific (14,750 men in 319 boats) made a disproportionate contribution to victory, but it also paid a high price for it — 3,500 men perished, and 52 submarines were lost.

USS **Wahoo**

When the legendary Dudley W. "Mush" Morton took command of the USS *Wahoo* (left) on the last day of 1942, he quickly turned the submarine into a finely honed weapon of war. During its historic third patrol in mid-January 1943, the *Wahoo* radioed in this report: "In ten-hour running gun and torpedo battle destroyed entire convoy of two freighters one transport one tanker…all torpedoes expended." When the sub arrived back in Pearl Harbor on February 7, 1943 — a broom lashed to its periscope signifying "a clean sweep" of enemy targets — her crew (above) was given a hero's welcome. From late April to late May, the *Wahoo* patrolled the East China and Yellow Seas. Although many ships were attacked, faulty torpedoes kept the score to only three sinkings. During August, in the nearly landlocked Sea of Japan, nine ships were attacked, without a single hit. In September, the *Wahoo* returned there for what was to have been a three-week stay. She never made it home. Japanese reports later listed a successful attack on an enemy submarine in the area — undoubtedly the *Wahoo* (official photos released by Japan in 2000 verify this). In an extraordinary combat career recognized with a Presidential Unit Citation, the USS *Wahoo* sank an astonishing twenty ships — despite faulty torpedoes.

USS **Tang**

The *Tang*'s skipper, Richard H. O'Kane, had served as Mush Morton's executive officer during his first months on the *Wahoo*, the best finishing school a submarine commander could have. After the *Tang* (below) arrived in Hawaii in December 1943, she quickly established an impressive record of successful attacks on Japanese vessels. On her first patrol, she sank four freighters and a tanker — scoring sixteen hits for twenty-four torpedoes fired. Her second patrol turned into a rescue mission, when she brought twenty-two downed US airmen to safety (above and left) during a three-day raid by US aircraft carriers on the Japanese base at Truk. In June and July 1944, the *Tang* executed a number of daring raids in the East China Sea, sinking ten ships. Late in September, the submarine began what would be her last war patrol. On the morning of October 24, 1944, in the Formosa Sea, the *Tang* attacked a Japanese convoy. After dispatching several merchant ships, and possibly a destroyer, the submarine closed on the last merchant ship in the convoy. She fired two torpedoes. One ran true — the other, her last, did not. It broached and curved around to the left, heading straight for the submarine. Of the sixty-six officers and men on board, only nine, including O'Kane, survived the sinking and subsequent hours in the water. They spent the rest of the war as prisoners, and O'Kane was later awarded the Medal of Honor. Although the *Tang*'s active career spanned just seven months, she sank a record twenty-four ships.

The Discovery of **I-52**

The Japanese submarine *I-52* lies 17,190 feet straight down in the Atlantic Ocean, 870 nautical miles from the Cape Verde Islands. Sunk in 1944 by American aircraft while carrying a load of rubber, tin, opium, quinine, tungsten, molybdenum and two metric tons of gold bullion, the 350-foot submarine was a link in the supply lifeline between Japan and Germany in the last year of World War II. For Paul Tidwell, a salvager from New Orleans, the *I-52* was a puzzle that became a passion. In 1998, after years of investigative work, Tidwell led an expedition to the wreck of the *I-52*, hoping to find the gold that was aboard it. The expedition brought to light fascinating photos of the lost sub, unseen for more than fifty years. But the sub's cargo of gold remained tantalizingly beyond reach, locked within its steel plating.

(Top) The *I-52*'s antiaircraft guns still point skyward, and the stern (above, left) lies largely undamaged, with its propeller guards intact. (Above, right) A remote submersible shines its light on the faded number 52. (Opposite) Rust adorns the windows of the conning tower and its surface radar devices. (Bottom) The *I-52*.

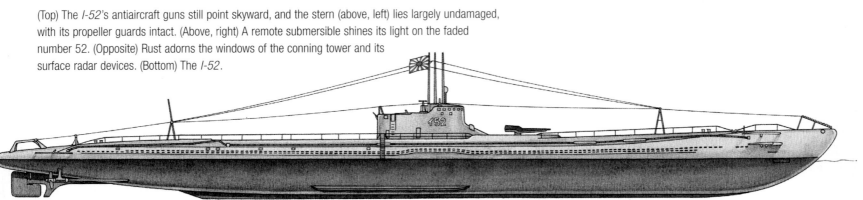

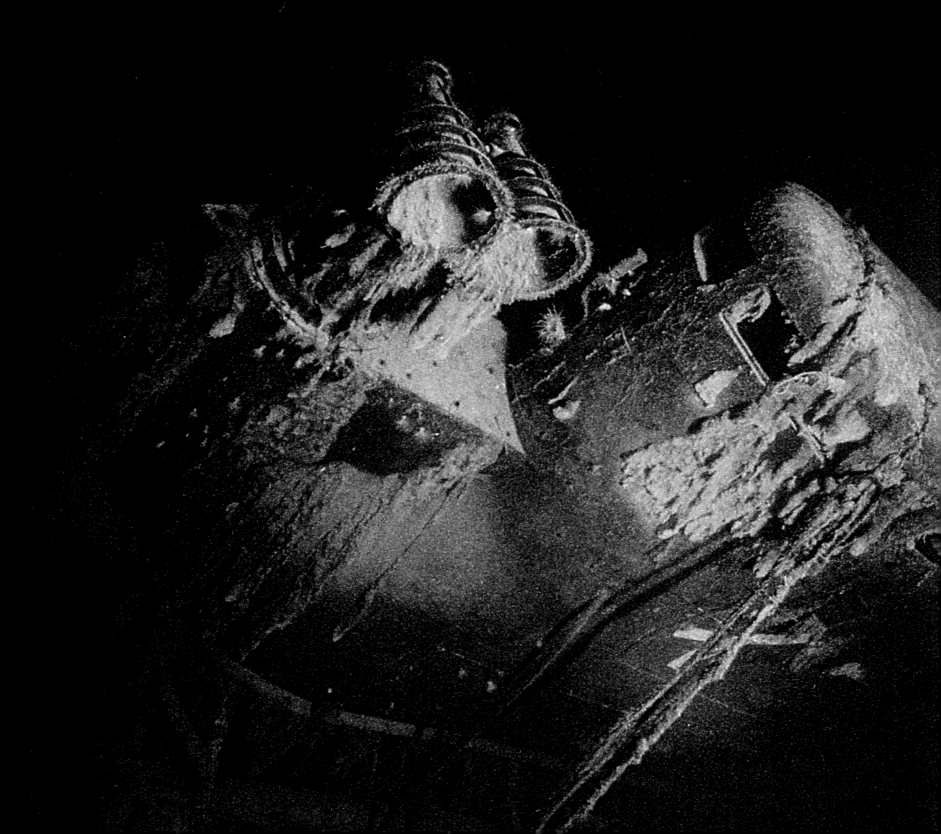

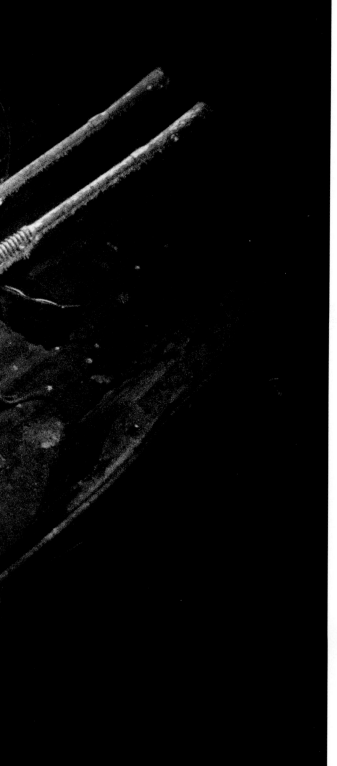

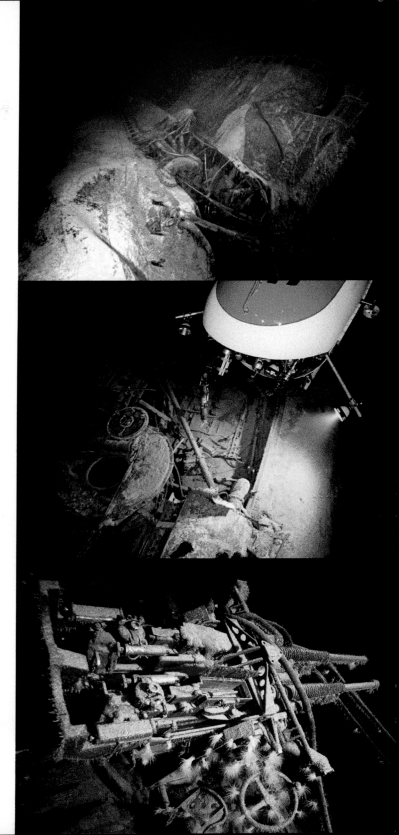

(Opposite, inset) The I-class cargo submarines, like these two and the *I-52*, were among the biggest in the world. *National Geographic* photographer Jonathan Blair accompanied Paul Tidwell on his expedition to the *I-52* and captured all the haunting images of the wreck featured here. (Opposite) The *I-52* stands on eternal patrol. (Below) Paul Tidwell holds some of the debris picked up from the site, including a scorched shoe (bottom). The *Mir* submersibles (*Mir-1* in photo at right) allowed the crews to document the full extent of the damage the *I-52* suffered after it was torpedoed by an Avenger airplane from the USS *Bogue*.

For some thirty years, until the Berlin Wall fell, NATO and Warsaw Pact submariners played cat-and-mouse games far beneath the surface of the world's oceans — their nuclear-powered craft bristling with weaponry, their sensors dedicated to finding out what "the other side" was up to. Officially, both sides were at peace. But deep within the cold waters of the Atlantic, North Pacific and Arctic, the "peace" sometimes got a little hot. In the early 1960s, the American submarine *Skipjack* hit a Soviet sub in the Pacific. In December 1967, the American nuclear sub *George C. Marshall* was clipped by a Soviet sub in the Mediterranean.

The submarine entered the atomic era in January 1955, when the USS *Nautilus* transmitted the historic message, "Under way on nuclear power." This was the vessel submariners had dreamed about for countless years — a true submarine, not merely a torpedo boat capable of making brief dives. As long as the fast new atomic submarines had enough supplies for the crew, they could stay submerged for months. In 1958, the *Nautilus* sailed right across the top of the world beneath the polar ice; in 1960, the *Triton*, another American atomic submarine, circumnavigated the globe without surfacing once. Ballistic missiles transformed the nuclear sub into *the* strategic naval weapon, supplanting the aircraft carrier. Other subs, sleek hunter-killers, shadowed these vessels — ready to attack them at any time.

Nautilus Heralds the Atomic Age

The nuclear-powered USS *Nautilus* (shown in New York Harbor on previous page) was built little more than half a century after the US Navy acquired its first submarine, USS *Holland*. During a twenty-five-year career that covered more than half a million miles, *Nautilus* shattered submerged speed and distance records and conquered the North Pole underwater. (Opposite, inset) First Lady Mamie Eisenhower christened the *Nautilus* on January 21, 1954. (Opposite, top) Albert K. Murray's watercolor of the *Nautilus*. (Bottom) a cutaway illustration. (Left) *Nautilus* commanding officer William R. Anderson informed President Eisenhower of the sub's arrival at the North Pole (far left).

1. Escape trunk
2. Engine control room
3. Steam turbine
4. Reactor
5. Attack center
6. Torpedo control center
7. Main ballast tank
8. Torpedo reloads
9. Torpedo tubes
10. Tethered marker buoy with telephone
11. Radar
12. Main engine room
13. Periscope
14. Snorkel

A Nation **Mourns**

When the American nuclear attack submarine USS *Thresher* failed to surface off the coast of Cape Cod on April 10, 1963, during deep-diving exercises, the nation was stunned. Two days later, as flags flew at half-mast throughout the country, the US Navy started its investigation into what had occurred some 5,500 hundred feet below the surface of the Atlantic. The *Thresher* had been heralded as the most advanced submarine in the world, capable of reaching speeds and depths never before imagined. It was equipped with state-of-the-art sonar and weapons systems. Yet despite all these technological innovations, at 9:18 A.M. on April 10, the *Thresher* broke apart — taking all 129 men on board to their deaths. Photographs taken by the bathyscaphe *Trieste* shortly after the wreckage was located document the catastrophic damage the nuclear submarine sustained. According to Dr. Robert Ballard, who photographed the impact site for the US Navy in 1984, "The *Thresher* looked as if it had literally been shredded — crushed by some giant, unseen hand." A court of inquiry ruled that a casting, piping or welding failure had flooded the submarine — shutting down all systems and sending the *Thresher* crashing to the ocean floor.

(Left, top and bottom) The *Thresher* during sea trials in 1961. (Inset) The submarine's insignia. (Above) The bathyscaphe *Trieste* is loaded for transportation to the site of the sinking. (Below) With the rescue ship *Preserver* in the background, the *Trieste* prepares for its first dive.

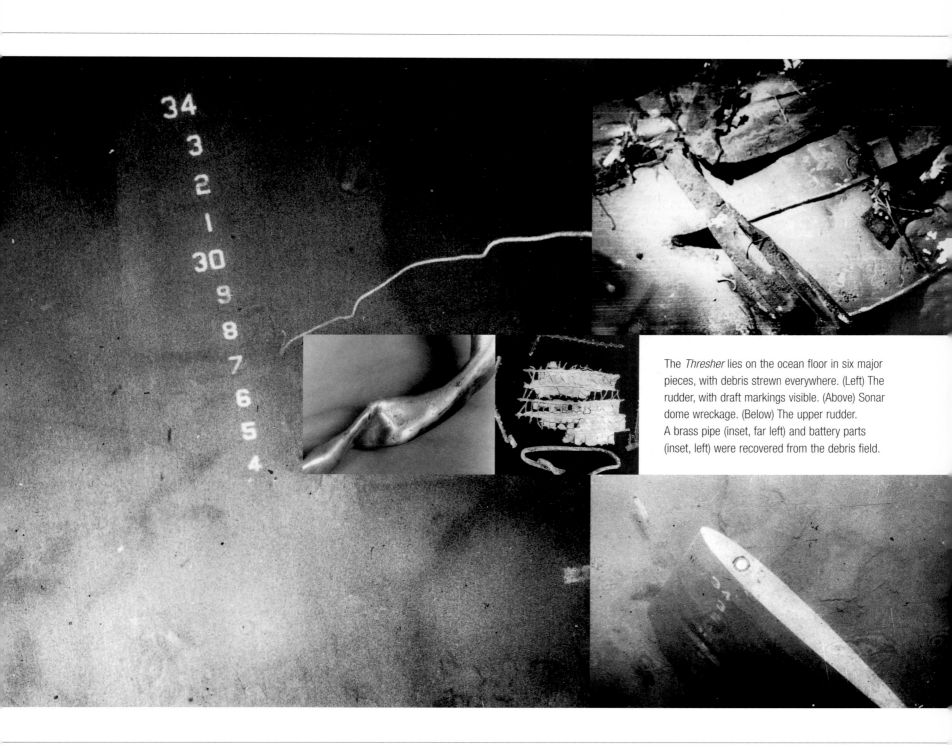

The *Thresher* lies on the ocean floor in six major pieces, with debris strewn everywhere. (Left) The rudder, with draft markings visible. (Above) Sonar dome wreckage. (Below) The upper rudder. A brass pipe (inset, far left) and battery parts (inset, left) were recovered from the debris field.

In May 1968, it looked as if all the undersea shadowboxing had at last claimed a victim. The 3,500-ton *Scorpion* failed to return to her base at Norfolk, Virginia. No emergency calls had been received from her, and there had been no reports from other vessels of anything untoward.

The *Scorpion* had been sent to the Mediterranean in March 1968 to take part in international navy exercises — in the role of a "bad guy," to be hunted by the antisubmarine forces of other friendly nations. It was a plum posting and included off-duty visits to many pleasant ports-of-call. But the crew was far from happy. In late April, after a stop in Naples, Italy, the men were informed of a change in plan; instead of going straight home, they were to proceed toward the Canary Islands. Their mission was to check on some odd activity by the Soviets involving large balloons. The suspicion was that the balloons might be equipped with electronic sensors for monitoring US nuclear tests.

After photographing the Soviet ships from a discreet distance for two or three days, the Americans had observed nothing unusual. With nothing to report, the *Scorpion* turned for home. She was taking a great circle track — the route taken by submarines through the North Atlantic — at a speed of eighteen knots. On the evening of May 21, a radio message reported that the submarine expected to arrive in Norfolk at 1 P.M. EST on May 27.

When the submarine didn't apppear on schedule, the navy had no reason to issue a general alarm; in all probability, the *Scorpion* was submerged and out of radio contact.

At Norfolk, waiting families were told that the submarine had been delayed. The wives, parents, friends and relatives had no inkling of anything amiss until newspaper reporters began contacting them. Everyone knew that the media only became interested in a story when they smelled trouble. The navy remained tight-lipped. The *Scorpion* was delayed, they kept saying in answer to the worried questions. There was no indication of a problem. Nothing to worry about. The glib words may have satisfied a few. But with no firm information forthcoming, rumors filled the vacuum.

Had she run afoul of the Soviets? After all, she'd been sent to shadow several of their ships (although exactly where these ships were remains uncertain). Two vessels — a submarine and a submarine rescue ship — had been conducting some kind of "hydroacoustic operation" southwest of the Canary Islands. The navy stated that "there were no observed changes in the pattern of operations of the Soviet ships, either before or after the *Scorpion*'s loss.…"

Others had their own suspicions about what might have befallen the submarine. "We have repaired, replaced or jury-rigged every piece of equipment," Machinist's Mate Second Class David

(Above) The USS *Scorpion* insignia. (Opposite) The submarine during sea trials in June 1960.

Burton Stone had written to his parents a few weeks earlier. Electrician's Mate Dan Rogers had demanded to be transferred off "USS *Scrap Iron*," as he and some of his shipmates called the vessel. According to them, she was months overdue for a major overhaul. Tight budgets and operational demands had delayed it. There were oil leaks in her hydraulic systems, and seawater leaks in her propeller-shaft seals. There was trouble with emergency ballast systems. Her dives had been restricted to a mere three hundred feet, about what the old-fashioned diesel submarines could manage. In late 1967, during high-speed maneuvers, the entire submarine had begun vibrating wildly. No one knew why — but everyone feared a recurrence of the problem, with God only knows what terrible consequences. Rogers' request for a transfer was not approved until he agreed to delete any reference to "danger" in connection with the *Scorpion*.

The possibility of a catastrophe haunted the navy. The sudden, unexplained silence, the lack of subsequent communication.... The dreadful possibility had to be faced: the 252-foot submarine, with her crew of ninety-nine officers and men, was probably lost.

(Above) John Craven, left, confers with senior navy officials during search operations.

The decision to bring in John P. Craven to assist in the search followed almost automatically. Two years earlier, Craven had found an H-bomb that had fallen into the sea off Palomares, Spain, after a collision between a B-52 and a tanker aircraft. Using startlingly original thinking, Craven had developed a map of the ocean floor in the region of Palomares — then called on his team of mathematicians to speculate on the bomb's location, using probability theory. Before any active searching began, Craven assigned numerical likelihoods to several locations. Although many people, including President Lyndon Johnson, thought Craven's scheme was completely bizarre, the missing bomb was eventually found precisely where Craven had calculated it would be.

Within a few days of the *Scorpion*'s disappearance, Robert A. Frosch, the assistant secretary of the navy for research and development, named Craven chairman of a technical advisory group to help find the missing submarine. A former navy man and head of the navy's Special Projects Office, Craven later wrote: "I realized that if we were going to find the *Scorpion*, the sounds of its collapse — the implosions that occur at collapse depth — would have had to have been recorded on some remote scientific or military hydrophone."

The United States Navy had a network of underwater listening stations called SOSUS (Sound Surveillance System) — but, unfortunately, these would not be of much help. Intended to pick up the faint whirrings and rumblings of Soviet submarines under the surface, they were also designed to filter out extraneous noises — including explosions.

With the help of civilian scientist Gordon Hamilton, Craven located a research station in the Canary Islands with an operational hydrophone. The machine routinely generated acres of paper covered with endless jerky pen marks that represented the underwater noises it picked up. Luckily, the mountains of paper generated around the time of the *Scorpion*'s disappearance were still there, awaiting disposal. Craven zeroed in on the data for two weeks in May. Sure enough, the lavish hills and valleys of the printouts showed five "separate trains of acoustic events that could have been associated with a submarine breakup." He noted the times of the "events" and, after comparing them with the submarine's speed and expected course, was able to establish eight locations where the *Scorpion* probably was at the time of these events. All eight were in waters at least two thousand feet deep. While the hydrophone data looked promising, Craven still had no proof that the blips on the printouts were, in fact, the *Scorpion*. The explosions could have resulted from countless causes, including illegal oil exploration.

Meanwhile, navy aircraft scoured the locations Craven had pinpointed, looking for wreckage or other evidence of disaster. They found nothing.

What Craven needed was corroboration. Ideally, if he could triangulate these explosions, he could plot their location precisely. The Naval Research Laboratory in Washington, DC, suggested checking two hydrophones in Newfoundland. These devices, located about two hundred miles apart, had been installed to track underwater shocks caused by Soviet nuclear tests. Wilton Hardy, head of the laboratory, sent for the records, all too aware that the chances of finding

Stealing a Soviet Submarine

Six weeks before the *Scorpion* disaster, the Soviet submarine K-129 disappeared off the coast of Hawaii. On board were three fully loaded nuclear missiles. The US Navy, which had been monitoring the submarine, was able to pinpoint its exact location — seventeen thousand feet below the Pacific. The CIA quickly realized that just outside its grasp was a fully armed Soviet submarine, filled with code books and other highly sensitive intelligence information. For everyone involved at the highest levels within the American government, it was immediately clear. The submarine must be retrieved from the ocean floor — at any cost, and with the greatest secrecy. Neither the Russians nor the American public must have any inkling that the United States was planning to steal a Soviet submarine.

Within months, President Richard Nixon authorized the largest covert operation since the Manhattan Project — and the vast sum of money needed to construct a state-of-the-art deep-sea salvage vessel. The operation's "cover" was the eccentric multimillionaire Howard Hughes and his company, Global Marine Development. Hughes announced construction of the Hughes Glomar Explorer, a massive salvage vessel to be used for recovering minerals from the ocean floor. What the public didn't know was that Hughes was also building a submersible mining barge, equipped with a secret giant "claw" for snatching the K-129 from the ocean floor.

The Glomar Explorer and the barge finally arrived on site in early July 1974. The claw — roughly the size of a football field — was lowered and latched successfully onto the sunken submarine. Halfway up, however, three of the arms suddenly gave way — and the K-129 broke apart. All that was salvaged by the CIA, according to later "official reports," was a single 38-foot section. To this day, there are conflicting versions about exactly what was found inside the Soviet submarine.

anything worthwhile were slim. The distances were too great — and the vast mid-Atlantic ridge of undersea mountains stood in the way. Would any sounds have penetrated that massive barrier?

The records were studied and they did provide something. But at first it was difficult to assess just what. They showed fluctuations that *could* have been the record of distant explosions. Or something else. Then Craven and his team added this data to what they'd learned from the Canary Islands hydrophone and the known facts of the *Scorpion*'s last voyage. Along the submarine's track, they could pinpoint two sounds that probably were explosions, ninety-one seconds apart — the second far louder and longer than the first. What caused the first, they couldn't say. But about the second,

(Left) The USNS *Mizar* (reclassified T-AGOR-11 in 1964) had also played an important role in locating and examining the wreck of the USS *Thresher*.

Craven and his fellow researchers now had no doubt. It was the sound of the *Scorpion* imploding.

Craven called the chief of naval operations, Admiral Thomas H. Moorer, and informed him that the awful possibility had almost certainly been borne out. The *Scorpion* was lost.

Understandably, Moorer demanded firmer evidence than wiggly blips on a printout before he would bring himself to release such shattering news. He demanded tangible evidence — wreckage, oil, fragments of bodies. He didn't get it. Nevertheless, a week later, he had to admit that the unthinkable had happened. The *Scorpion* was indeed missing, her crew probably dead.

But what had caused the tragedy? Until that was known, every nuclear submariner would worry that a similar fate was awaiting his boat. It was vital that Craven and his team find the *Scorpion* — and the cause of her sudden, violent death.

The navy sent in an oceanographic survey ship, the USNS *Mizar*, under the direction of the Naval Research Laboratory. Its commander was Chester "Buck" Buchanan, a civilian oceanographer. A tenacious tracker, Buchanan began growing a beard the day the *Mizar* left port, declaring that he would not shave until he had succeeded in his mission. He initiated his search by circling over Point Oscar, the location of the first explosion. Finding nothing, Buchanan turned west, since that was the direction in which the submarine had traveled.

At the same time, Craven kept poring over his data, looking for anything that might help the *Mizar* in her quest. Then he noticed something startling: in her last moments, the *Scorpion* had not been heading west. She had been heading *east,* back toward the Mediterranean. Was she being pursued?

Craven asked several submarine captains why a submarine would suddenly head east when its destination was west. They all gave the same grim answer: a submarine makes a 180-degree turn if it experiences a "hot run" (an active torpedo on board a sub). For submariners, no prospect is more frightening than being hit by your own torpedo, something that happened a number of times in the Second World War. Modern submarine torpedoes were designed to shut down if they suddenly turned during launch. The same safety device worked even if the torpedo was still on board.

The *Scorpion* carried a full complement of torpedoes: fourteen Mark 37s, seven Mark 14s, and two Mark 45 Astors equipped with nuclear warheads. Her skipper, Lieutenant Commander Francis A. Slattery, would have ordered "right full rudder" at the first mention of trouble from the torpedo room. In fact, the *Scorpion* had survived just such an emergency only six months earlier.

Inquiries revealed that several submarines had experienced hot runs because electrical leads in the onboard equipment used to test the torpedoes had not been connected correctly. Craven was certain the same thing had happened aboard the *Scorpion* — but this time, the hot-running torpedo had exploded. Many of his colleagues weren't so sure. (Bottles of scotch were wagered on the point.) Craven next had a ship drop small explosive charges at Point Oscar, to compare the "acoustic signature" with those of the original explosions. The evidence indicated that the *Scorpion* was, indeed, heading east — and at a greater speed than Craven had first thought.

Craven then set up a computer simulation, with the *Scorpion*'s former executive officer, Lieutenant Commander Robert Fountain, taking the helm. Fountain was told only that he was heading home at eighteen knots — then he received the sudden alert, "Hot-running torpedo!"

Fountain didn't pause. "Right full rudder," he ordered immediately. It was the automatic response, one drilled into all submarine commanders. Next, Craven simulated an explosion. Fountain followed routine — blowing ballast, pouring on speed, trying to save his sub. Ninety seconds later, the submarine passed the critical depth of two thousand feet. It imploded, squashed by the crushing pressure

(Above) The *Scorpion*'s commanding officer, Francis A. Slattery, had assumed command of the nuclear-powered attack submarine only the previous October.

of the ocean. This tallied with the series of noises Craven had picked out of the hydrophone data.

Craven now set out to develop a mathematical chart of the ocean floor, using methods similar to those employed in finding the missing H-bomb off the coast of Spain. He asked submarine and salvage experts to bet on the probabilities presented. How fast was the submarine going when it imploded? The consensus was between forty and forty-five knots. Was the *Scorpion*'s crew trying to contend with a hot-running torpedo? Aware that the submarine had changed course and was heading east at the time of her disappearance, the group then considered the probable glide path of the stricken vessel. She might have nosedived straight to the bottom. Or her trajectory might have been far less acute; she could have traveled as far as seven feet forward for every foot she went down. The majority felt that she probably traveled some three to four feet forward for every foot she dropped. After sifting through a veritable Everest of data, Craven concluded that the *Scorpion*'s remains would probably be found east of Point Oscar, four hundred miles from the Azores, on the edge of the Sargasso Sea.

The navy didn't agree. The *Mizar* had come across a few fragments the navy believed belonged to the *Scorpion*. But nothing more was found. The weeks passed. October arrived with high winds and heavy seas. The navy wanted to terminate the investigation. Buchanan pleaded with Craven to persuade the naval authorities to wait a little longer. Craven succeeded in getting him another two weeks.

Exactly one week later, Craven received a cryptic message: Buchanan had shaved his beard.

The date was October 29, 1968 — five months since the *Scorpion* had been declared missing. Its remains had been located less than one-eighth of a mile from where Craven had calculated they would be. The submarine had broken almost in two; only a small hinge-like piece of metal connected the sections. The forward hull, which included the torpedo room and most of the operations compartment, had gashed a massive trench in the ocean floor when it hit. The aft hull section, including the reactor compartment and the engine room, had created a second trench. The propeller and shaft had been ripped out of the hull.

Craven held to his "hot run" theory. But a 1969 court of inquiry declared that the loss of the *Scorpion* "remained a mystery" and that no "incontrovertible proof of the exact cause" could be found. The same year, the navy sent down a deep-sea submersible, *Trieste II*, to study the wreck at close quarters. The examination revealed no evidence of an attack or an external torpedo hit. The hull adjacent to the torpedo room appeared to be intact, whereas the battery well was almost totally destroyed. There the matter rested.

Various search and detection equipment was mounted on a towed sled (above) used by the *Mizar* during its search for the *Scorpion*. (Opposite) This view of the sunken submarine's bow section was taken by a deep-submergence vehicle shortly after the wreckage was located, at a depth of over ten thousand feet.

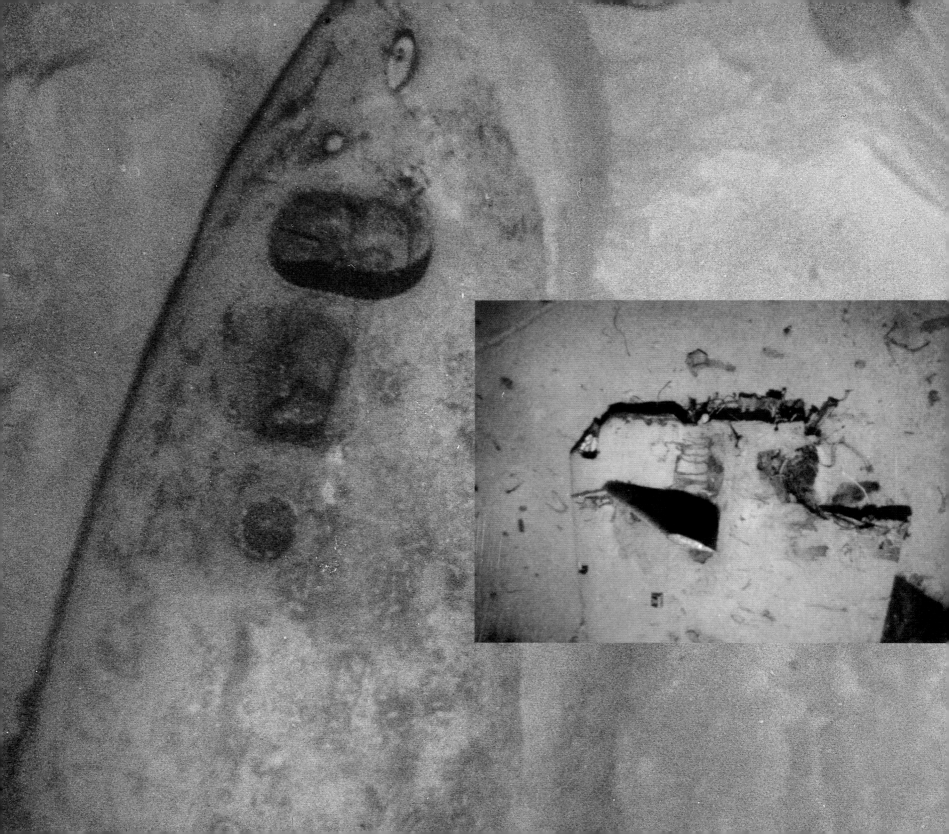

Revisiting the **Scorpion**

In 1985, oceanographer Dr. Robert Ballard and a team from the Woods Hole Oceanographic Institution secretly took photographs of the *Scorpion* wreckage as part of a classified US Navy effort to survey the debris. Ballard was already in the Atlantic, in search of another famous lost ship — RMS *Titanic*. These images were first made public in 1993, when the navy started declassifying information about the *Scorpion* disaster. (Opposite) An overhead view of the bow section of the submarine. (Inset, opposite) The detached sail, with a large after section missing. Debris is scattered about. (Inset, middle) The after messenger buoy cavity. (Inset, right) A stern view, showing the upper portion of the rudder. (Bottom) One of the last photographs of the *Scorpion*, taken in April 1968 when the sub tied up alongside the USS *Tallahatchie County* outside Clayton Harbor in Naples, Italy.

(Above) The top of the hull, aft of midships, taken shortly after the *Scorpion* was found. The large oval opening is the stowage bay for the messenger buoy. Also visible are circular ballast tank vents, two rectangular access hatches into the superstructure and damaged snorkel exhaust piping.

More than twenty years passed. Then in the early nineties, Craven received an unexpected telephone call from Charles M. Thorne, former technical director of the Weapons Engineering Center in Keyport, Washington — now retired, as was Craven. The two men had never met. Thorne had a question for Craven: Had he seen a classified alert issued in 1968 describing the failure in tests of an MK-46 battery designed for use on Mark 37 torpedoes? The alert described how a torpedo battery had exploded in flames during a vibration test. It was the most violent failure the lab had ever experienced. Three engineers narrowly escaped with their lives. Black, choking smoke billowed from the test mechanism. Chemical extinguishers could do little to tame the upheaval. While technicians were frantically trying to unbolt the battery from the shaker, it exploded again, drenching them in the potassium hydroxide that was the battery's electrolyte. The sixteen-gauge steel battery case was peeled open like a sardine can. The alert recommended that all batteries from that production lot be

150   LOST SUBS

"withdrawn from service at the earliest opportunity." It added that sufficient heat was generated in the test sample "to risk warhead cook-off (a low-level explosion) and the loss of a submarine."

Incredibly, the bulletin had never been sent to Craven — and the *Scorpion* was lost only days after its publication.

Production of the batteries had initially been awarded to two manufacturers. But their batteries suffered so many failures that a third manufacturer was brought in. The third company never succeeded in producing any batteries that could pass the navy's quality tests — but because of a chronic shortage of batteries, the company received permission to ship some two hundred and fifty of them.

It was one of these batteries that exploded during the laboratory test. But the blame couldn't be attributed to the manufacturer. The basic design of the battery was at fault. Engineers had repeatedly asked the navy to redesign the battery. But the navy, committed to supplying torpedoes in large numbers, wouldn't even consider such a move. A redesign would take many months, perhaps years. The existing batteries simply had to be made to work.

The problem lay in a tiny component, a fragment of etched foil worth a cent or two. It controlled the flow of electrolyte into the power cells. The foil was supposed to break with pressure; the battery then took over, providing power for the torpedo's motors. In the laboratory, intense vibration made the electrolyte push against the thin diaphragm with insufficient force to break the foil. But enough electrolyte leaked into the battery's power cells to cause sparking and overheating — which, in turn, could set off a warhead.

With the last grim piece of the puzzle in place, it is easy to imagine the scene aboard the *Scorpion* during her last moments. Perhaps the submarine's earlier vibration problem had reoccurred, setting off a torpedo. The captain would have swung the ship hard starboard at the first word of torpedo trouble. But this was no hot run. The torpedo exploded in a small blast, what is called "a low-level explosion." A fire may have broken out. Or perhaps the blast popped the external hatches in the torpedo room. As the *Scorpion* flooded, she dived ever deeper — until she reached collapse depth.

In the final moments, her pressure hull would have bulged inward, then she would have imploded — with a blast of heat and a shock wave that killed every man aboard almost instantly. Implosion would have followed rumbling implosion as compartment after compartment flattened inward. From beginning to end, her terrible death would have taken about three minutes.

About a year after the loss of the *Scorpion*, Naval Ordnance finally ordered a redesign of the battery.

Bringing the **Dakar Home**

When the bridge of the Israeli Navy submarine *Dakar* was raised by the Nauticos expedition team from the bottom of the Mediterranean Sea in October 2000, it marked the conclusion of a gripping underwater search mission that had begun thirty-two years earlier. In early January 1968, the *Dakar* — a modernized World War II T-class submarine purchased by Israel from the Royal Navy — departed Portsmouth, England, with a crew of sixty-nine men for the journey home to Haifa. On January 28, just east of Crete, the submarine transmitted a request to enter port. It was the last known contact with the *Dakar*. Despite an immediate air and sea search, no trace of the submarine was found — until a year later, when one of its

(Left) In January 1968, as Britain's flag is lowered and Israel's raised, HMS *Totem* becomes INS *Dakar*. (Above) The ladder and trunking leading to the bridge, photographed at the wreck site. (Insets) The *Dakar*'s after emergency marker buoy (top) and the recovered bridge ladder (above).

(Right) The bridge of the *Dakar*'s conning tower on the seafloor, with the gyro visible at bottom. (Top) A close-up of the gyro. (Above) The recovered section superimposed by Nauticos onto a 1968 photograph of the *Dakar*.

emergency beacons was found half-buried on a beach in Gaza. Twenty-five separate expeditions were eventually launched to find the missing submarine. All ended in failure. Finally, in 1996, after the Israeli Navy consulted with US Navy experts, it decided to concentrate its search efforts along the *Dakar*'s route from Portsmouth to Haifa — an area overlooked during all previous expeditions. And it hired US-based Nauticos Corporation to undertake the mission. Using the latest sonar search systems and the REMORA 6000 remotely operated vehicle, the search team located and identified the *Dakar* on May 28, 1999 — ten thousand feet below the surface of the Mediterranean between Cyprus and Crete. The following year, the expedition returned to the site to conduct a forensic investigation into the possible causes of the sinking — and to recover the detached forward section of the conning tower. The *Dakar*'s conning tower had been customized with a ten-man escape trunk equipped with a ladder, to allow divers to exit the submarine through the bridge while submerged. It was this feature that had aided in positive identification of the wreckage. Brought back to Haifa, the bridge will be incorporated into a memorial honoring the crew of the *Dakar*. In spirit, at least, the *Dakar* had finally made it home.

Chapter Eight: **Disaster under the Barents Sea**

The *Kursk*'s length and enormous size are evident in photographs taken of the submarine in the Barents Sea (above) and docked at the naval base in Vidyayevo (opposite). (Inset) Captain Gennady Lyachin.

Captain Gennady Lyachin was immensely proud of his ship, the nuclear submarine *Kursk*. With a surface displacement of approximately 14,000 tons, she was one of the largest, most powerful submarines in the world, probably the finest of the "superweapons" developed by the Russians in the post-communist era. The 505-foot-long, Oscar II-class submarine (an SSGN, or nuclear guided-missile submarine), compared favorably with the best the Americans had produced — with excellent performance and, by Russian standards, superb crew quarters.

In the summer of 2000, the *Kursk* (named for the great Soviet tank victory over the Germans in 1943) was ordered to take part in a thirty-ship exercise in the Barents Sea, northeast of Murmansk. The forty-five-year-old Lyachin was elated; these were to be the biggest Russian naval maneuvers in years, and the perfect opportunity to show off the capabilities of his ship.

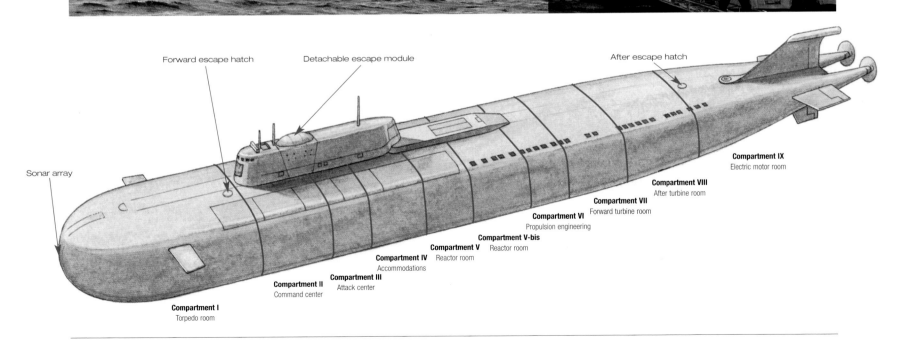

Sonar array

Forward escape hatch

Detachable escape module

After escape hatch

Compartment IX
Electric motor room

Compartment VIII
After turbine room

Compartment VII
Forward turbine room

Compartment VI
Propulsion engineering

Compartment V-bis
Reactor room

Compartment V
Reactor room

Compartment IV
Accommodations

Compartment III
Attack center

Compartment II
Command center

Compartment I
Torpedo room

By noon on August 12, the *Kursk* had completed a successful torpedo-firing run. Aboard the submarine, the crew prepared for a second run. Lyachin radioed the task-force commander requesting permission to fire. Two hundred miles away, the American surveillance vessel USS *Loyal* was monitoring the transmission and heard the commander give his okay. Operators expected the sound of torpedoes. Instead, they heard only a short, sharp explosion — followed within a few minutes by an "enormous, thundering boom." According to a Norwegian seismic institute that recorded the explosions, the second registered 3.5 on the Richter scale, carrying the force of two tons of TNT.

In a fraction of a second, a routine exercise had become a catastrophe. The *Kursk*'s forward section disintegrated, flooding her torpedo compartment. The intricate maze of pipes and valves, gauges and controls that gave her life had been reduced to a tangle of scrap metal. In the forward compartments, every officer and crewman was dead, their lives snuffed out in the blink of an eye. In the control room — the vessel's nerve center — Lyachin and his key officers perished too, incinerated in the unimaginable heat of a flash fire followed by the gigantic pressure wave that demolished everything in its path. The vessel's first four compartments were obliterated instantly. Massive, watertight bulkheads may have kept the sea from the two VM-5 pressurized water reactors that powered the *Kursk*, at least for the moment. But death would have come quickly for crewmen in the reactor control rooms and the turbines, for the boat tipped, nose down, its steam turbines still delivering power until the automatic shutdown. A few seconds later came the cataclysmic collision with the seabed — the scream of steel ripped and torn, the crushing of machinery, the fracturing of a thousand components in the darkness 354 feet below the surface. Robbed of power and light, save for the wan light generated by the emergency electric power system, the submarine sank into the sea mud like a huge monster burrowing in to die.

Crammed into the ninth compartment (which housed the rear escape chamber), twenty-three members of the crew were still alive, still struggling to come to grips with this terrifying reality. The temperature in the *Kursk* dropped rapidly. Agonizing headaches began to afflict the men as the level of carbon dioxide rose and the atmosphere became increasingly foul. As the hours ticked away, the crewmen sank into a surreal state — logical thought giving way to mindless lethargy, consciousness slipping slowly into coma as life ebbed away, one man at a time.

Lieutenant-Captain Dmitry Kolesnikov, commander of the submarine's turbine section, waited along with his shipmates. He was bitterly cold and knew there was little chance that rescue would

(Above) The submarine's commemorative badge. (Opposite, top) Captain Lyachin, right, and the crew of the *Kursk* during a naval parade in Severomorsk on July 30, 2000. (Inset, left) The crew on the deck of the *Kursk* in early summer 2000 — and (inset, right) leaving the submarine in October 1999, after a trip to the Mediterranean Sea. (Opposite, bottom) A diagram of the *Kursk*, showing the division of its ten compartments.

come in time to save anyone. Earlier, in what little emergency light remained, he had made a list of all twenty-three men still alive then. Now, painstakingly, in the dank darkness, he wrote a farewell note to his wife Olga, whom he had married only a few weeks before. He carefully wrapped both notes in plastic in the hope that they would survive. Within a few hours of penning the message to his wife, Kolesnikov was dead.

What had caused the disaster?

The Russians, as always, seemed unwilling to divulge any details. For the first two days, they said nothing at all. Then they issued a statement declaring that the submarine had suffered "a technical fault" and was lying on the seabed. Later, Defense Minister Igor Sergeyev proclaimed that there was "incontrovertible evidence" that the submarine had collided with another vessel. If so, responded the United States immediately, it was not an American vessel.

On August 16, four days after the *Kursk* sank, the Russians changed their story; they now admitted there *had* been an explosion in the weapons area of the submarine. Western experts tended to agree, speculating that the explosion could be attributed to a torpedo (the *Kursk* could carry as many as twenty-eight), a missile (the submarine usually carried twenty-four cruise missiles), or a high-pressure tank of the type used to blow ballast water when surfacing. Alternatively, the submarine might have hit a mine, perhaps one left over from the Second World War — although at first glance, it seemed improbable that a mere mine could have caused such damage to the fortress-like *Kursk*. Possibly, an explosion in the battery compartment was to blame. Again, though, the sheer extent of the devastation seemed to point to some other, more potent cause.

Despite this, Deputy Prime Minister Ilya Klebanov still maintained that the *Kursk* had hit "a huge, heavy object" of "very large tonnage" and that the collision had torn open the submarine's hull. But Klebanov offered no suggestions as to what the "huge object" might have been. And no reports of damaged ships were forthcoming from any country.

In the West, opinion was almost universal that the Russians themselves were probably responsible. While still bent on presenting a modern, technologically sophisticated face to the world, they have consistently underfunded the navy — and, indeed, all branches of the services — except for those involved in politically significant actions, such as the war in Chechnya. Compounding the problem was the sadly inadequate training of crewmen and the generally poor quality of senior staff.

By August 17, the *Kursk* tragedy dominated headlines in Russian newspapers (above) — even as President Vladimir Putin (top) tried to play down the gravity of the situation. (Right) Deputy Prime Minister Ilya Klebanov, second from right, answers questions during a press conference.

In the years since the end of the Cold War, the Russian Navy has shriveled in size by more than eighty percent (Western navies have declined about forty percent in the same period). From a peak strength of more than six hundred vessels, the Russians now have fewer than one hundred — and only about ten percent of those are fit for sea duty.

The *Kursk* was the navy's showpiece, constantly at sea while the rest of the nuclear fleet sat rusting in dock — their indifferent crews more concerned about the likelihood of their next paycheck arriving than about the serviceability of their vessels. It was a vicious circle. Poor maintenance meant that the ships could put to sea only rarely. This, in turn, led to insufficient training, particularly relating to emergencies and rescue operations.

Perhaps Vladimir Putin couldn't be blamed for looking dumbfounded when he learned of the tragedy. Soon after assuming the presidency from the jocular but ailing Boris Yeltsin, Putin, anxious to rebuild morale, had declared his intention of bringing the Russian Navy up to the levels of the British and French fleets. The exercise in which the *Kursk* was lost was intended as a dress rehearsal for a show-of-force cruise in the eastern Mediterranean led by the carrier *Admiral Kuznetsov* and

(Left) A still from Russian television shows the rescue ship *Rudnetsky* and its mini-sub during initial rescue efforts. (Top) Norwegian divers aboard the diving ship MV *Seaway Eagle* (above) test their equipment in preparation for their descent to the *Kursk*.

the battle cruiser *Peter the Great* — with the *Kursk* as the showpiece. Now, with her loss, the popular Russian leader had suffered a stinging setback. Despite the catastrophe, however, Putin decided not to cancel the start of his summer vacation at Sochi. Later in the week, at a gathering of visiting academics, he responded to reporters' questions — admitting that the situation was "critical" but declaring that every step was being taken to rescue the crew.

Westerners were skeptical. For several days, the Russians had rejected all offers of assistance from the United States, France, Britain and Norway. Meanwhile, RTR, the Russian state-owned television network, continued to broadcast a day-by-day summary of the tragedy. With the sort of brazen disregard for the truth that has become so familiar in Russian governmental communications, RTR amended the chronology of the tragedy to create a story of an efficient rescue operation in order to placate the growing disapproval of the Russian people. But the various branches of the government didn't take the trouble to get their stories straight. RTR reported that rescue operations began late on August 13 — despite the fact that Commander Igor Dygalo, the navy's official spokesman, had previously announced that the main rescue operation had already started. The RTR further claimed, on

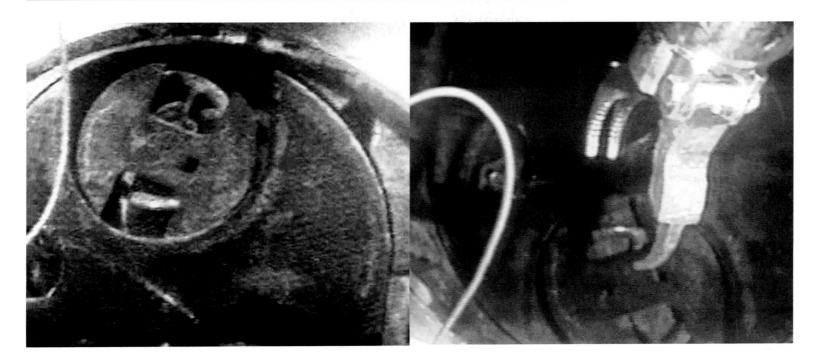

(Above, left) A television still of the *Kursk*'s escape hatch and (right) the mechanical arm used by Norwegian divers to wrench it open.

the fifteenth, that the navy had accepted Western offers of help. Despite this pronouncement, on the sixteenth, Deputy Prime Minister Klebanov assured the Russian public that no foreign help was needed; the Russian Navy had all the necessary equipment to effect a rescue.

On August 15, in fact, the Russians attempted to lower a submersible vessel to the *Kursk*. The effort was frustrated because the submarine was lying at an angle on the seabed, preventing a proper mating of the submarine and the submersible. The Russians made several more attempts, each one ending in failure because of strong currents and the position of the wreck. On the eighteenth, a Russian rescue capsule succeeded in latching onto the submarine briefly — but damage to the hatch prevented a secure docking. With each failed attempt, the hope of rescuing any survivors continued to fade.

On Saturday, August 19, the Norwegian ship *Seaway Eagle* arrived from Aberdeen, Scotland, carrying several divers and a remote-controlled camera. The divers had been sent by the multinational offshore contractor Stolt Offshore, to aid in rescuing any of the *Kursk*'s crew who might still be alive. On August 20, they reached the stricken submarine.

"The hope at the beginning was that we were going to get somebody out alive," said Alistair

A Husband's
Undying Love

Lieutenant-Captain Dmitry Kolesnikov and his wife Olga (above) were part of a tightly knit submariners' community in Vidyayevo that included several other recently married couples. Shortly before the *Kursk* departed on its ill-fated last voyage, Olga and several other wives had joined their husbands for a relaxing day-long visit aboard the Russian submarine. The photo above was taken that afternoon. Fun-loving and easygoing, Dmitry — or Dima, as he was known to family and friends — also kept several photos of Olga taped to the control panels in the turbine section over which he proudly presided (inset). On August 12, as Kolesnikov sat huddled with the other survivors, his thoughts were with his family, and with his beloved wife. Using his pet name for her, he began a note he knew she would read only after his death: "Olechka! I love you! Do not suffer too much!" Olga finally read the note in October, shortly after her husband's body was recovered from the *Kursk*.

Clark, one of the divers. "It would have been nice to be able to do so but it wasn't to be." Once the first hatch was opened, it became obvious that the submarine was completely flooded and no one had survived.

According to the Russian Navy, the accident did not result in abnormal radiation levels in the Barents Sea.

Not until late October were divers able to enter the *Kursk* and begin the grisly task of removing the remains of the crew. One of the first bodies to be brought out was that of Dmitry Kolesnikov. The note he had written to his wife Olga was discovered in one of his uniform pockets, still wrapped in plastic. It read, in part: "13:15. The whole crew of the sixth, seventh and eighth sections have moved into the ninth. There are twenty-three of us here. We made this decision [to move back as a result of the accident]. None of us has been able to get out." He had added a chilling footnote: "I am writing in pitch blackness."

It appeared the survivors of the initial explosions did not die instantly, as the Russians had stated on several occasions. The rapping sounds that had been heard from the submarine in the first days after the sinking could have been collapsing equipment or the settling of the vessel into the seabed — or the frantic banging of trapped sailors. Four of the bodies showed signs of severe burns; others were "heavily deformed" and had clearly suffered from the blows of sharp and blunt objects. A Russian spokesman said, "It seems that as everything was falling apart, they were hit both in the head and in the body."

Olga Kolesnikov claimed that her husband had experienced a premonition of death before leaving on his last voyage. She said her husband gave her a strange goodbye when he left home: he had written a poem to her, talking of death and love.

The mourning began (left) shortly after the *Kursk* sank, as families of the missing crewmen were taken to the site of the disaster. It continued in November 2000 (above), during state funerals honoring the first victims recovered from the stricken submarine. And it swelled again during memorial services on August 12, 2001, at Vidyayevo (far left), where the crew was based.

Russian and international salvage experts felt the *Kursk* should be raised, although the job would probably take several months and would cost up to half a billion dollars. Other suggestions included refloating the submarine using cables attached to platforms or huge air floats, dismantling it underwater or leaving it where it sank and hermetically sealing it with a biological gel to prevent any radioactive leakage.

In May 2001, the Russians signed a deal with the Dutch company Mammoet — specialists in heavy lifting and transport — to raise the *Kursk*. Mammoet's partner in the *Kursk* salvage operation, Dutch maritime expert Smit International, would handle all underwater work. It was decided to cut away the submarine's mangled torpedo compartment first and leave it and its still-dangerous torpedoes on the ocean floor, to be dismantled later.

In order to raise the truncated hull, twenty-six holes were drilled through the outer and inner hulls, and specially designed plugs were inserted. Like massive toggle bolts, the plugs — each designed for a specific location on the hull — expanded once they had passed through the holes. A 459-foot barge, the *Giant 4*, dropped anchor directly over the sunken *Kursk*, bringing twenty-six computer-controlled lifting jacks to bear on the massive job of bringing the 18,000-ton hull to the surface. To handle the gigantic weight, each of the immensely strong cables was made up of fifty-four steel strands.

Raising the Massive Kursk

Weighing almost 24,000 tons underwater — and lying approximately 350 feet below the surface of the chilly Barents Sea — the massive Russian submarine presented a formidable challenge to the two Dutch companies charged with bringing it to the surface and back to dry dock. The operation was undertaken in several stages.

❶ Secured by hydraulic cylinders positioned on either side of the sub, a remotely controlled giant cutting chain severed the sixty-five-foot-long damaged front section — which is scheduled to be retrieved by the

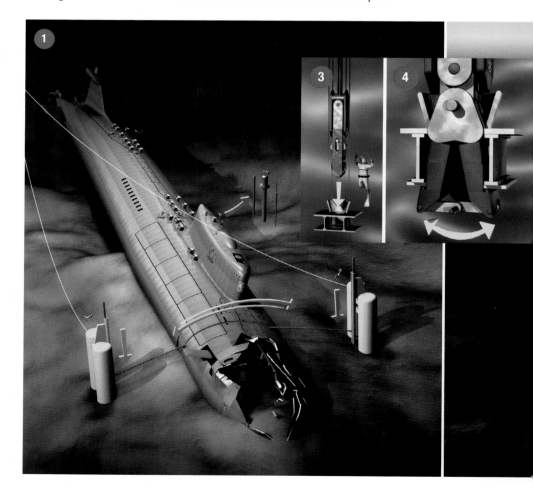

Russians in summer 2002. The periscopes and antenna were also removed. Divers then used high-pressure water jets to cut holes through the outer and inner hulls along the length of the sub. ❷ The *Giant 4* barge, fitted with sophisticated lifting equipment — and with its hull modified to hold the raised sub — was positioned above the *Kursk* by eight lines anchored to the seabed. Once all holes had been cut, heavy-duty lifting cables ❸ were lowered from the barge to the submarine and anchored into the holes with specially designed plugs. Once each plug was inserted, its arms unfolded under the beams and the inner skin of the sub

— anchoring the plug securely to the structure ❹. The lifting was precisely controlled, with the force on each bundle of cables set individually to minimize the tension on the *Kursk*'s hull. ❺ When the *Giant 4* arrived in Roslyakovo, two water-filled pontoons were attached alongside in preparation for getting the barge and sub into dry dock. ❻ In dry dock, the water was pumped out of the pontoons as the vessels were maneuvered into position. ❼ After the the barge and pontoons were removed, the dock holding the sub was towed to another shipyard — where a careful examination of the wreckage began.

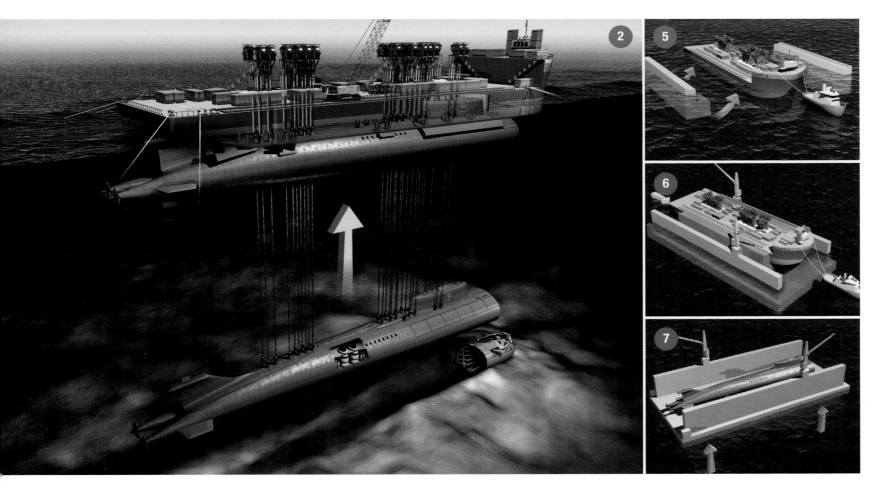

The twenty-six lifting jacks, operating in unison, raised the hull at a rate of some thirty-three feet per hour. Once the *Kursk* was firmly attached to *Giant 4*, the barge was towed by a tug to Roslyakovo, where two water-filled pontoons were attached, one on either side. Water was pumped out of the pontoons, lifting the submarine so it could fit into the dry dock. The final stage was the removal of the *Giant 4* and the pontoons — leaving the remains of the submarine in dry dock for examination and eventual scrapping.

In the days that followed the *Kursk*'s arrival in the sealed-off shipyard at Roslyakovo in late October 2001, Russian officials began their painstaking investigation into the possible causes of the

(Below left) Air bubbles from the *Kursk* as massive steel cables lift it from the bottom of the Barents Sea. (Below) Workers adjust the pontoons before easing the *Kursk* into dry dock. (Bottom) The gutted wreckage of the submarine.

(Below) Only the conning tower is visible as the *Kursk* floats in the dry dock at Roslyakovo. On the front of the submarine is Russia's state emblem, and on the side is the emblem of the city of Kursk.

massive explosion aboard the nuclear submarine — and dealt with the somber task of removing the remaining bodies of the crewmen. President Putin, still smarting from fierce public criticism of his initial handling of the *Kursk* disaster, had promised that all bodies would be recovered and buried with full honors.

On March 23, 2002, in a moving ceremony in St. Petersburg attended by approximately one thousand mourners, Russia buried the last recovered victims of the *Kursk* tragedy — including the submarine's captain, Gennady Lyachin. As the investigation into the explosion aboard the *Kursk* continues, attention has focused on a faulty torpedo as the possible cause.

What Sank the **Kursk?**

Throughout the rescue attempts and for many months after, the Russian government stuck to the collision theory — although its spokesmen also hinted briefly of sabotage by Chechnyan-sympathizing crewmen. Collision was a politically attractive scenario (intrusive foreign submarines menacing gallant Russian sailors) and it was supported by statistics that chronicled twenty-five such collisions in the Barents Sea since 1967. But the United States denied any involvement, and none of their submarines had reported any damage.

A very different possibility — made public for the first time in a BBC TV documentary aired in August 2001 — emerged from an unlikely quarter: a tiny hamlet called Blacknest, deep in the quiet English countryside. A British government seismic monitoring station located there had picked up the *Kursk* explosions on its equipment thousands of miles away. What the seismographs recorded were two "blips" — the first, fairly small; the second, far larger. But what was most extraordinary about these two "events," according to the researchers at Blacknest, was their similarity. What they showed was not a collision followed by an explosion, but *two* explosions — a small one, and then a much larger one.

But what had caused the two explosions? As researchers struggled for an answer, a disaster that had befallen another submarine almost half a century earlier provided an important clue.

In 1955, the British submarine *Sidon* sank after an explosion in Portland Harbor on England's south coast. Thirteen men were killed. The *Sidon* had on board two experimental torpedoes that motion while a torpedo was being reloaded during a preparation drill. Then the safety device designed to prevent the flow of HTP failed and the fuel got into the engine-starting circuit. Had the torpedo been launched and under way, its running engine would have relieved the sudden buildup of heat and pressure caused by the mixing of HTP with a catalyst. But the weapon was sitting in its tube. Within seconds, the stainless steel tube containing the HTP ruptured, and the entire supply poured into the torpedo's body. The HTP encountered a contaminant, which ignited the concentrated superheated oxygen — and a massive explosion occurred.

Although the nuclear-powered *Kursk* was a very different vessel from the *Sidon*, the two submarines had one thing in common: both carried torpedoes that used HTP. Perhaps, researchers speculated, what had happened aboard the *Sidon* had also occurred aboard the *Kursk*. The Russian submarine was conducting practice torpedo firings and had probably fired at least one torpedo. Perhaps another torpedo had been activated accidentally and the HTP exploded, starting an intense fire.

However, since the practice torpedoes aboard the *Kursk* would have been fitted with dummy heads, not warheads, any initial explosion would have been confined to the HTP only. Yet the massive damage done to the *Kursk*'s sixteen-inch-thick

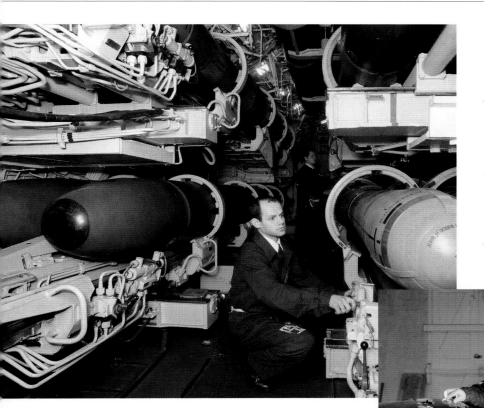

(Above) The torpedo room of an Oscar-class Russian submarine. (Right) Torpedo expert Maurice Stradling was the first to draw parallels between the *Sidon* and *Kursk* tragedies in a BBC TV documentary. (Opposite) A computer-generated image of the *Kursk* explosion, courtesy of BBC TV.

used hydrogen peroxide (HTP) as an oxygen and heat source for the torpedo engine. Colorless and odorless, HTP resolutely refuses to ignite even in the presence of a naked flame. But when it comes into contact with a suitable catalyst, it turns into oxygen and superheated steam — and its volume increases dramatically, as much as five thousand times.

In the *Sidon*'s case, two things went gravely wrong. First, the sequence that starts the torpedo engine was accidentally set in

pressure hull suggests that quite a few torpedoes went off simultaneously. So far, the Russians have not revealed how many torpedoes the nuclear submarine was carrying, nor what type. They have, however, conceded the danger of HTP torpedoes and it is believed they have taken them out of service.

While the HTP theory is a tantalizing one, it has raised more questions than answers. The official investigation into the sinking continues.

Epilogue: **For Those in Peril**

The sea has never been safe. Nor will it ever be. The risks that submariners take are those of any sailors at any time — albeit of a much higher order. Conventional sailors face their dangers upon the water; a submariner's environment envelops him and is ready at any moment to reassert its supremacy.

Yet in the aftermath of each undersea disaster, submarines have become safer. Tragedy has spurred the development of innovative concepts such as personal rebreathing equipment, the submarine rescue chamber, compartment and tower escape systems, personal survival equipment and the Deep Submergence Rescue Vehicle — greatly increasing the chances of survival if trouble does occur. But the prospects of avoiding a catastrophe are better also. At the time of writing, no American or British submarine has been lost in over thirty years. In fact, submarines are now perceived to be so safe that a number of companies manufacture civilian submarines — and find a ready market for their craft.

If the risks have been minimized, the benefits remain as great as ever — as great as when the idea of a ship capable of sailing undetected under the water first occurred to Alexander the Great. In the aftermath of September 11, 2001, the submarine was once again a key strategic player as British and American nuclear submarines, equipped with Tomahawk cruise missiles, hit Taliban targets deep within Afghanistan with pinpoint accuracy — and total impunity.

Those who serve in submarines are well aware of the risks they face — and from the *H.L. Hunley* onward, there has been no shortage in the world's navies of those brave enough to ask for this strenuous duty. They push their ships, and themselves, to the utmost, in peace or in war (of either the cold or hot variety).

Those twisted wrecks that lie mute on the world's seafloors are a tribute to the daring and courage of what is referred to as The Silent Service.

Index

Bibliography

Ackerman, Paul. *Encyclopaedia of British Submarines, 1901-1955.* Munsingen, Switzerland: Paul Ackerman, 1988.

Botting, Douglas and the editors of Time-Life Books. *The U-boats.* Amsterdam: Time-Life Books, 1979.

Blair, Clay. *Hitler's U-boat War, Volume 1: The Hunters, 1939-1942,* and *Volume 2: The Hunted, 1942-1945.* New York: Random House, 1996, 1998.

Brenchley, Fred and Elizabeth. *Stoker's Submarine.* Sydney: HarperCollins Publishers, 2001.

Compton-Hall, Commander Richard. *Submarine Boats: The Beginnings of Underwater Warfare.* London: Conway Maritime Press, 1983.

Craven, John P. *The Silent War: The Cold War Battle Beneath the Sea.* New York: Simon and Schuster, 2001.

Dönitz, Karl. *Memoirs: Ten Years and Twenty Days.* New York: Da Capo Press, 1997.

Gray, Edwin. *Few Survived: A History of Submarine Disasters.* London: Leo Cooper, 1986.

Kaplan, Philip and Jack Currie. *Wolfpack: U-boats at War, 1939-1945.* London: Aurum Press Ltd., 1997.

Kemp, Paul J. *The T-Class Submarine: The Classic British Design.* London: Arms and Armour Press, 1990.

Lenton, H. T. *Navies of the Second World War: American Submarines.* Garden City, NY: Doubleday & Company Inc., 1973.

Perkins, J. David. *The Canadian Submarine Service in Review.* St. Catharines, Ontario: Vanwell Publishing, 2000.

Preston, Antony. *Submarine Warfare: An Illustrated History.* London: Brown Books, 1998.

Ragan, Mark K. *The Hunley: Submarines, Sacrifice, and Success in the Civil War.* Miami/Charleston: Narwhal Press Inc., 1995, 1999.

Rössler, Eberhard. *The U-boat: The Evolution and Technical History of German Submarines.* Translated by Harold Erenburg. London and Melbourne: Arms and Armour Press, 1975.

Sontag, Sherry and Christopher Drew with Annette Lawrence Drew. *Blind Man's Bluff: The Untold Story of Submarine Espionage.* New York: Perennial, an imprint of HarperCollins Publishers, 2000.

Tarrant, V. E. *The U-boat Offensive, 1914-1945.* Annapolis, MD: Naval Institute Press, 1989.

van der Vat, Dan. *Stealth at Sea: The History of the Submarine.* London: Orion Books Ltd., 1995.

Websites

Dakar — Bringing the *Dakar* Home
www.nauticos.com

Dakar —Dolphin-Israeli
Submariners Association
www.dolphin.org

Dictionary of American Naval Fighting Ships
www.hazegray.org

Discovery of the *AE2* (Royal Australian Navy)
www.navy.gov.au

Fleet Type Submarines On-line
www.maritime.org

Friends of the Hunley
www.hunley.org

John Philip Holland and his Submarines
www.geocities.com

Kursk Catastrophe —
Russian Naval Museum
www.museum.navy.ru

Kursk Salvage —
Mammoet and Smit International
www.mammoet.com

Lieutenant Otto Weddigen's Account
of the *U-9* Submarine Attack
www.lib.byu.edu

Naval Historical Center (for information and
photographs on US submarines —
including the *Squalus*, *Thresher* and *Scorpion*)
www.history.navy.mil

Peacetime Submarine Accidents
www.lostsubs.com

Royal Navy Submarine Museum
www.rnsubmus.co.uk

Submariner's Association, Barrow in Furness
Branch (includes excellent articles on the *Perseus*,
Totem and *Truculent* submarines)
www.submariners.co.uk

U-boat Archive
www.uboatarchive.net

U-boats — World War I and World War II
www.uboat.net

There are also many other excellent
websites dedicated to specific submarines and
submariners' associations.

Picture Credits

Every effort has been made to correctly attribute all material reproduced in this book. If any errors have unwittingly occurred, we will be happy to correct them in future editions. Copyright is held by the institution, individual or photo agency listed.

All illustrations, unless otherwise noted, are by Jack McMaster.

AKG — AKG Photo
AP — AP/Wide World Photos
BCM — Bettmann/Corbis/Magma
H|A — Hulton|Archive/Getty Images
HDC — Hulton-Deutsch Collection/Corbis/Magma

Magma — Magma Photo News
ME — Mary Evans Picture Library
NA — National Archives
NHC — Naval Historical Center
RNSM — Royal Navy Submarine Museum

Front cover (top) and 2–3: Painting by
Claus Bergen, courtesy of AKG Berlin
Front cover (bottom): Brian Skerry
Back cover: Brian Skerry with Ira Block
1: Painting by Stephen Bone, War Artists
Collection, National Maritime Museum
4–5: Brian Skerry
7: Jonathan Blair/National
Geographic Society
8: Painting by Claus Bergen, Collection
of the National Maritime Museum
10–11: Reuters NewMedia/
Corbis/Magma

CHAPTER ONE

12: Electric Boat Corporation
14: (top left) Art-Tech; (top right) ME;
(bottom) The Art Archive/
Smithsonian Institution/
Eileen Tweedy
15: (left) Library of Congress;
(right) ME
16–17: ME

CHAPTER TWO

18–19: The Museum of the Confederacy
20: (top) NA; (bottom) NHC
21: BCM
22: NHC
23: (top and bottom right) Daniel
Dowdey; (bottom left) Library of
Congress, courtesy of the South
Carolina Institute of Archaeology and
Anthropology
24–27: Daniel Dowdey
28: National Park Service Submerged
Cultural Resources Unit
29: (left, top and bottom) with the kind
permission of Friends of the Hunley;
(right) Christopher F. Amer, with the
kind permission of Friends of the
Hunley

30–31: Brian Skerry with Ira Block
32: (bottom) with the kind permission
of Friends of the Hunley
33: Christopher F. Amer, with the kind
permission of Friends of the Hunley
34–36: with the kind permission of
Friends of the Hunley
37: Daniel Dowdey

CHAPTER THREE

38–39: HDC
40: ME
41: (top) The Mariners' Museum/Corbis/
Magma; (bottom left) Art-Tech;
(bottom right) BCM
42: BCM
43: Brown Brothers
44–45: RNSM

CHAPTER FOUR

46: AKG
47: AKG Berlin
48: H|A
49: (top) AKG London; (bottom)
courtesy of uboat.net
50: (left) H|A; (inset) AKG; (cutaway)
Art-Tech
51: (left) Corbis/Magma; (right) AKG
52: (top left) Painting by Felix
Schwormstadt, courtesy of Bildarchiv
Preussischer Kulturbesitz; (top right
and middle) Corbis/Magma
53: (top) Library of Congress; (bottom)
BCM
54: H|A
55–57: Paintings by Ken Marschall
58: Brown Brothers
59: H|A
60: AKG Berlin

61: (top) Imperial War Museum;
(bottom) Painting by Achille
Beltrame, from *Domenica del
Corriere*, Rizzoli Periodici, Milan
62: Painting by C.R. Fleming-Williams,
The Art Archive/Collection of the
Imperial War Museum
63: (left) H|A; (right) Corbis/Magma
64: (left) NA; (top) NHC;
(above) Captain John Chatterton;
(bottom) Art-Tech
66: (left) BCM; (right) Corbis/Magma
67: Corbis/Magma
68–69: Painting by Charles Bryant,
courtesy of Australian War Memorial
69: (inset) Australian War Memorial
70: (top) Mark Spencer; (inset)
Australian War Memorial
71: Mark Spencer

CHAPTER FIVE

72: Richard Quilter/BCM
74: ME
75–77: NHC
78: (top) BCM; (bottom) AP
79: NHC
80: (inset, left) AP; (inset, top right)
BCM; (inset, bottom right) HDC;
(bottom) NHC
81: (top) The Illustrated London News
Picture Library
82: Brown Brothers
83: (top) Corbis/Magma; (bottom)
Portsmouth Naval Shipyard
photograph, Milne Special
Collections and Archives, University
of New Hampshire Library
84: (top right) AP; all others NHC
85: AP
86–87: RNSM
88: (top) H|A; (inset) Corbis/Magma
91: (right) RNSM

92: H|A
93: (top left) H|A; (right and bottom left) RNSM
94: RNSM
95: (top left) RNSM; (right and bottom left) BCM

CHAPTER SIX

96–97: Painting by John Hamilton, Collection of the Imperial War Museum
98: (top) Corbis/Magma; (bottom) H|A
99: (left) ME; (right, top and middle) Corbis/Magma; (bottom right) H|A
100: (top) HDC; (inset, left) AKG London; (inset, right) H|A
101: Painting by Randall Wilson, with the kind permission of Cranston Fine Arts
102: H|A
103: (top) Corbis/Magma; (bottom) Art-Tech
104: AKG London
105: Lawson Wood/Corbis/Magma
106: NHC
107: (left) HDC; (right) AKG London
108: HDC
109: AKG London
110–111: Painting by John Hamilton, Collection of the Imperial War Museum
112: RNSM
113: Kostas Thoctarides/AP
114: NA
114–115: Painting by Anthony Saunders, with the kind permission of Cranston Fine Arts
117: (top left) BCM; (top right) Painting by James W. Kerr, courtesy of the Museum of the City of New York; (bottom) NA
118: Brian Skerry; (inset) NA
119: Brian Skerry
120: AKG London
121: (top left) Corbis/Magma; (bottom left) Australian War Memorial; (right) HDC
122: Corbis/Magma
123: (top) NA; (bottom) Art-Tech
124: Painting by Lieutenant Leonard Frank Brooks, Collection of the Canadian War Museum
125: (top left) BCM; (bottom left) Corbis/Magma; (right) H|A
126–127: Painting by Dwight Clark Shepler, NHC Art Collection
127–129: NHC

130–131: Jonathan Blair/National Geographic Society
132: Priit J. Vesilind and Jonathan Blair; (inset) NA
133: (right) Jonathan Blair; (insets) Jonathan Blair/National Geographic Society

CHAPTER SEVEN

134–135: Brown Brothers
136: (letter) Eisenhower Library; (inset) NA
137: (top) Painting by Albert K. Murray, NHC Art Collection; (inset) Brown Brothers; (bottom) Art-Tech
138: (bottom right) BCM; all others NHC
139–141: NHC
142: courtesy of John P. Craven
144–150: NHC
152: (top) Nauticos Corporation; (left) Dolphin-Israeli Submariners Association; (top right inset) Uri Dotan, Dolphin-Israeli Submariners Association; (bottom right inset) Nauticos Corporation
153: (bottom left) Uri Dotan; (right and top left) Nauticos Corporation

CHAPTER EIGHT

154: Corbis/Magma
155: AP
156: (top, and left inset) Reuters NewMedia/Corbis/Magma; (right inset) AFP/Corbis/Magma
157: Reuters NewMedia/Corbis/Magma
159: (top left) AP; (bottom left) AFP/Corbis/Magma; (right) Alexander Zemlianichenko/AP
160: (left) AP/RTR; (right) AP/SCANPIX
161: AP/RTR
162: (top) AFP/Corbis/Magma; (inset) Reuters NewMedia/Corbis/Magma
163: (top) Dmitry Lovetsky/AP; (bottom left) Pool, Sergei Karpukhin/AP; (bottom right) Reuters NewMedia/Corbis/Magma
164–165: Art by Joe Lertola, ©2001 Time Inc.
166: (left) AP/Pool; (right) AFP/Corbis/Magma
167: AP/Pool
168: courtesy of Horizon/BBC TV
169: (top) Corbis/Magma; (inset) courtesy of Horizon/BBC TV
170–171: Brian Skerry

Acknowledgments

Madison Press Books is indebted to a number of people for their invaluable help during the course of this project. Special thanks to our technical consultant, David Perkins, who tirelessly responded to our many queries and provided excellent data and references whenever needed; and to Jack McMaster, whose original illustrations and diagrams are featured throughout the book. We would also like to thank the following for vetting specific chapters of the book and for providing help during the research and writing of the original manuscript: Christopher Amer, South Carolina Institute of Archaeology and Anthropology; David and Lynn Jourdan, Nauticos Corporation; Dr. Mark Spencer; and Larissa van Seumeren, Mammoet.

We would like to acknowledge and thank Debbie Corner of the Royal Navy Submarine Museum and Janea Milburn of the Naval Historical Center for their endless patience and tireless help in researching and providing a large number of the historical images featured here.

Our warm thanks to photographers Jonathan Blair and Brian Skerry, who generously provided their underwater images for our use. We are also grateful for the many hours they both devoted to this project. Our thanks as well to Daniel Dowdey, for allowing us such generous access to his *Hunley* art; and to Joe Lertola, who created the art for the *Kursk*.

Lastly, we are also indebted to Kellen Butler, for Friends of the Hunley; Dean Jacobowitz and Neil Ruenzel, Electric Boat Corporation; Richard Jeffery, BBC TV Picture Archives; Tina Poitras, Magma Photo News; John Rutter, National Geographic Society; and Marcia Skerry.

Editorial Director: Hugh Brewster

Associate Editorial Director: Wanda Nowakowska

Project Editors: Wanda Nowakowska, Laurie Coulter

Manuscript Editor: Ian Coutts

Editorial Assistance: Lisan Jutras

Photo Research and Acquisition: Donna Chong, Susan Aihoshi

Art Director: Gordon Sibley

Graphic Designer: Nathan Beyerle

Illustrations and Diagrams: Jack McMaster

Production Director: Susan Barrable

Production Manager: Donna Chong

Color Separation: Colour Technologies

Printing and Binding: SNP Leefung Printers Limited

LOST SUBS was produced by **Madison Press Books**.